THE
IMPACT
EQUATION

THE IMPACT EQUATION

Are You Making Things Happen or Just Making Noise?

Chris Brogan and Julien Smith

Portfolio / Penguin

PORTFOLIO / PENGUIN
Published by the Penguin Group
Penguin Group (USA) Inc., 375 Hudson Street,
New York, New York 10014, U.S.A.
Penguin Group (Canada), 90 Eglinton Avenue East, Suite 700,
Toronto, Ontario, Canada M4P 2Y3
(a division of Pearson Penguin Canada Inc.)
Penguin Books Ltd, 80 Strand, London WC2R 0RL, England
Penguin Ireland, 25 St. Stephen's Green, Dublin 2, Ireland
(a division of Penguin Books Ltd)
Penguin Group (Australia), 707 Collins Street, Melbourne,
Victoria 3008 Australia (a division of Pearson Australia Group Pty Ltd)
Penguin Books India Pvt Ltd, 11 Community Centre,
Panchsheel Park, New Delhi – 110 017, India
Penguin Group (NZ), 67 Apollo Drive, Rosedale,
Auckland 0632, New Zealand (a division of Pearson New Zealand Ltd)
Penguin Books, Rosebank Office Park, 181 Jan Smuts Avenue,
Parktown North 2193, South Africa
Penguin China, B7 Jiaming Center, 27 East Third Ring Road North,
Chaoyang District, Beijing 100020, China

Penguin Books Ltd, Registered Offices:
80 Strand, London WC2R 0RL, England

First published in 2012 by Portfolio / Penguin,
a member of Penguin Group (USA) Inc.

1 3 5 7 9 10 8 6 4 2

LIBRARY OF CONGRESS CATALOGING-IN-PUBLICATION DATA

Brogan, Chris.
The impact equation : are you making things happen or just making noise? /
Chris Brogan and Julien Smith.
p. cm.
Includes index.
ISBN 978-1-59184-490-7
1. New products.   2. Creative thinking.   3. Internet marketing.
4. Entrepreneurship.   5. Social media.   I. Smith, Julien.   II. Title.
HF5415.153.B75 2012
658.8'72—dc23   2012027307

Printed in the United States of America   •   Set in Sabon   •   Designed by
Jaime Putorti

To Violette and Harold.
You're the best thing I was ever a part of, and
I look forward to learning more from you.
—Dad

To Helen.
—JS

Contents

Ceci n'est pas un social networking book.

This Book Is About More Than Social Networks

The actor James Cagney appeared in well over fifty films, achieving numerous awards, including the Oscar for best actor. The American Film Institute put him in the top ten of its 50 Greatest Screen Legends.

Cagney played tough guys, and if someone tries to imitate him, they will likely sneer, cock their head, and say, "Why, you dirty rat!" perhaps while erupting into fake machine-gun fire. If you're old enough, you may even remember a reference in *Home Alone*, the 1990 film starring Macaulay Culkin as an eight-year-old fighting two bumbling burglars trying to enter his home on Christmas Eve. You can probably hear the Cagney sound bite now: "Keep the change, you filthy animal."

But here's the thing. Cagney never actually said, "Mmmmm, you dirty rat" or "Why, you dirty rat" or even "You dirty rat, you killed my brother." Near as anyone can tell, the closest Cagney ever got to the phrase was "Come out and take it, you dirty, yellow-bellied rat, or I'll give it to you through the door!"

In a way, we feel like Cagney. We don't feel that we focus on how amazing and wonderful social media are, but people often cite us when they talk about social media or list us as authorities on social networks. Well, you dirty rats, read on, because we've got more than that up our sleeve.

You might have picked this book up thinking it's about social media. That's fair. We wrote a *New York Times* best-selling book that people also thought was about social media and social networks, until they read it. People may say the same about this one.

The Impact Equation is actually about getting a larger audience to see and act upon your ideas and learning how to build a community around that experience to take it all to an even higher level.

When we talk about this, we mention the tools we use to build our platform. Yes, these tools are often social networks. But looking at *The Impact Equation* as if it were a book about social media is like saying *Moby-Dick* is a book about boats. The tools *do* define some of the milieu. We *do* mention that it's much easier to build a platform using social-network tools than it was when one had to rely on the attention of the mainstream media.

But that's not the topic. The topic is *impact.* This book will explain how to build ideas, how to move them through a platform so they will be seen and discussed, and then build a strong human element around those ideas so people actually know you care about their participation.

It feels a bit strange to continue rehashing this point. Lance Armstrong said, "It's not about the bike." No one ever asked Hemingway what kind of typewriter he used to write his stories—well, they probably did, but you see our point.

We're not writing about Twitter and Facebook and Google+ and Pinterest and Path, because who cares? Those things are temporary, and they aren't the things that matter. The people are what matters. Are you with us?

PART **1** Goals

1 Working with the Impact Equation

"There are two types of people in this world," Brett Rogers said. "You're either a head of lettuce or an apple tree.

"Look, if you want to grow lettuce, you plant your seeds, give a little water, and two or three months later you can make yourself a salad. But that lettuce will spoil soon after it reaches maturity, and good luck trying to save it for the winter, let alone find another use for it other than your burger or Caesar salad.

"I look at my life and my approach to business as that of the apple tree. It takes about six years for an apple to grow from a seed into an apple-producing tree. That's a long time even in human years. You have to take care of that tree during those six years too, with no guarantee it will make it to maturity. But you know what? At around the six-year mark, that apple tree starts producing apples, and with a little care and a bit of luck that tree could produce apples for well over a hundred years. And apples keep way better than lettuce. Plus, you can make apple juice, apple cider, apple pie, and all sorts of other foods.

"So am I special? No. I just kinda think of myself as an apple farmer, and so I just gotta keep tending the trees until they provide the fruit."

#

Brett Rogers is an adventurer with an amazing story. If you haven't heard of him yet, don't worry. You'll be happy you did now.

Most people who watch a bit of television know adventurers like Bear Grylls and Les Stroud. If they read some books, they might know Wade Davis, the great traveling anthropologist, or maybe David Suzuki. Most don't yet know Brett Rogers, but one day they probably will.

You could call Brett a riverboat captain. He's a big guy, almost like a bear, and he's surprisingly young for someone who's gone on so many adventures. He traveled down the Mississippi and the Yukon rivers on boats free of any fossil fuels—basically epic, glorified rafts. These trips take months, and along the way he documents his process, creating films that help others understand the rivers he loves so much.

How Brett created his career is fascinating, and hearing him talk about his trips is cool, but the most intriguing part is that, ten years ago, his career couldn't have existed.

Brett's job is totally new. He isn't actually paid to travel down these rivers. He isn't paid by television executives, *National Geographic*, or the Discovery Channel—well, sometimes he is—but that's not really what happens. What actually happens, the way it really works, is that he's paid by people like you and me.

Brett's job isn't like that of most documentary filmmakers or even adventurers. Most of these people need to win grant money or borrow from what they call the "3 *F*s" (friends, family, and fools). Then, once a filmmaker has funding, he goes out, makes his movie, and then tries to sell it. But not Brett.

He cares who watches his films, of course. He cares about the rivers he travels and about the executives who buy the rights to show his films on television, but his real audience, the people he really cares about, are more committed than that: They are the people who decide they want to go along with him. Here's how he tells it.

"When I was eighteen, a buddy and myself took a four-day bus trip from Toronto to the Yukon Territory. We ended up hiking an eighty-kilometer trail through Kluane National Park. We crossed raging rivers and hiked over mountains covered in snow. I had always been obsessed with the Yukon since I was a child, thanks to a *National Geographic* documentary, *Yukon Passage*, and the writings of Canadian author Pierre Berton. The Yukon was all I had imagined and more, but on the trip home we traveled by ferry through the panhandle of Alaska, and then we hitchhiked across British Columbia before ending up in Jasper. Having just experienced the wilds of the Yukon, I was deeply disturbed by the development of Jasper. Sure, Jasper was a beautiful town, but Jasper was a national park, not Alberta's answer to Disneyland. I was disturbed.

"I set off for university with the inclination that I knew I wanted to do something that could make the world a better place. The years rolled on by, and the effects of a lifetime of being institutionalized were beginning to dull my spirit; I knew I had to get back to the wilderness. Long story short, one weekend in October of 2003 I had my eureka moment—I was going to build a raft and travel the Mackenzie River.

"I was a geography major at the University of Waterloo, and my facility had video cameras that students could rent out for a few days at a time for projects. I figured since I was going so far north I should make an effort to document the experience, so I ended up pulling some strings and got a brand-new video camera purchased through an endowment fund with permission to borrow the camera for the summer. I set off for the Northwest Territories with some friends, my sister, and a video camera in late June of 2004."

They ended up with forty-four hours of footage, and eight months later he sold the rights to *Into the Midnight Sun* to the

Documentary Channel in Canada. It premiered in front of hundreds of people at the University of Waterloo.

It was after this premiere that a surprising thing happened: Dozens of people began to approach Brett, asking him to go on his next expedition. He figured, why not build a raft and take it down the Yukon now? He fired off an e-mail making the offer to everyone who had said they wanted to come. He named his price, and eight people agreed. This funded his next documentary in its entirety, and in May 2006, they all headed for the Yukon Territory. His next adventure had begun. He hadn't been anointed or given the golden touch by some TV station. He didn't need them. He had picked himself.

#

We first heard the story of Brett Rogers at a local event where he spoke about his adventures. We were inspired—what he was doing was different. He wasn't asking permission from anyone before he went out, and he didn't need any major organization to do it. Brett just decided to leave on his own, figuring it out as he went along. This is something any entrepreneur can get behind, no matter what adventure they're on. The leap out into the unknown is understood by anyone who takes a chance.

In a way, all those who take that risk are brothers and sisters. We're all part of the same tribe. We understand that ventures mean you have to put yourself out there, into the unknown. Whether it's big or small, your project needs attention, and it needs supporters, and it needs help. Adventurers of all stripes understand this.

But the interesting part is this: Though Brett may be trying to make movies to impress a larger audience, the expedition mates who go along with him are his real clients. Only after the fact do the products of his efforts go on to impress people in the production and film industries, as well as "interesting, powerful people in general," as Brett would say. He has done something interesting, something most never even think of doing, so as he connects to the larger public, his exploits precede him and his ability to have an impact expands.

But the real point isn't about Brett at all. In a sense, Brett's story is also your story. Brett loves rivers. He writes about them, travels them, and documents their changes. But we want you to think about your unique contribution and how it belongs in the world of the twenty-first century, where everything is worldwide and instantaneous—a world of YouTube and Twitter and a billion other channels. We want you to think about how your tribe can come from anywhere. We want you to think about how to leave an impression on those who matter and help them gather around you. We want their passion and yours to come together so that you can leave your mark on the world.

In short, we want you to have an impact.

#

Look, we're in a time of change. One hundred years ago, fifty years ago, even twenty-five years ago, the world of media was nothing like it is today. This is a unique time.

It's a time when ideas can spread, maybe for the first time ever, based not on who created them and how important or rich that person is but instead on how good the idea is. A quote, a meme, or a strong emotion can pass through a network of people faster, effecting political change, creating art, or even making people feel closer than ever before. Ideas can help people change the world, and now anyone can become powerful enough to be a catalyst for what matters to them.

There are fewer restrictions on connecting with the ones who matter and speaking to them directly. This is one reason (of many) that we personally feel lucky to be alive. In another world, a long time ago, people just like us talked about their ideas at parties, in their homes, with their friends, but those ideas got nowhere. The ideas died before they had a chance to reach the people who mattered. Today, we talk about them online, where they can change people and, hopefully, help make their lives better.

So what's unique about this book isn't that it exists but that two people like us wrote it. We aren't special. In another time period we would have had nine-to-five jobs with great benefits and no upward mobility. The infrastructure of that time period would have restricted us—now the infrastructure sets us free. We were given opportunity simply because of when we were born and where we happened to be.

But this doesn't apply only to us. There are fewer excuses than ever. So if you've delayed making something of your own or bringing a long-lost idea to life for the first time, congratulations, now is the time to do it. It is perhaps the best time possible, because the barriers are lower than they ever have been.

A good idea now gets less resistance from media, because there are no longer five channels but five billion. Good ideas don't have to pass through ABC, NBC, CNN, the *New York Times*, or anything else you recognize before they get to you. An idea may, in fact, go through no outlet you recognize whatsoever, until it suddenly connects with you on Facebook, on Google+, or elsewhere.

We are more platform agnostic than ever. Coming to a new Web site, you may trust it or you may not, but you care much less about where an idea originates and much more about who shared it with you. Our media world is a far cry from listening exclusively to Dan Rather on *CBS Evening News*, and this is largely because we all get to be a part of it.

In a sense, this is a book about how to be the best medium you can be, whether you are an individual, a small group of upstarts, or a giant organization. It was created in bits and pieces from knowledge we have picked up about what works and what doesn't, what's significant and what can be forgotten. It comes from our successes and our failures.

It needs to exist because most people have not been to journalism school or studied to be writers or marketers, and yet everyone must be all of those things. We have all these hats by necessity, not by talent. So more than ever, we need a highly diverse set of competencies that will help us get out there, help us brand ourselves, and help our businesses succeed.

Not everything we write is holy writ, but we have worked hard to make sure that what we talk about is based on principles. Because this book is about spreading ideas and making your mark, we have made sure that it can apply equally across any medium, whether you're on the social Web or shouting to a crowd in a public square.

We can do this because, at their core, all people influenced by ideas are the same, whether they connect to the idea through Facebook or television. Instead of talking about the medium, we talk about the people and give you some metrics to help reach them effectively. That is why this book is designed around an equation. It's about the things that matter for you, to get through to the people you care about.

#

We both naturally understand the technology of social networks, but it isn't what we care about and it isn't how we really build our businesses. We don't think about optimizing the location of the Twitter button or getting the maximum number of retweets or Facebook likes. There are experts who think about this, but we aren't them. What we think about, at the end of the day, is people.

No matter what happens, whatever the change in technology, people will always stay the same. Whatever, whether they watch one screen or five to relax in the evening, the way people think will always be based on same brain they, their parents, and their grandparents were born with. Working with and thinking about the human dimension has always served us well because it means we understand the final recipient.

So, we have never been that interested in mathematical notions of popularity or influence, like Klout scores or numbers of followers. It has always been more important to us to develop a connection with a single person, and to know how to do that well, than to do it en masse.

When we developed the Impact Equation, this is what we were thinking about. We were considering what mattered to the person on the other end of the line. We considered what would make a difference to that final individual who connected with an idea and how he or she would perceive it.

In some ways this is easier, because you're thinking about only one person; but in other ways it's complex, because who knows what a single person is thinking? That challenge is what the Impact Equation became about.

$$\text{Impact} = C \times (R + E + A + T + E)$$

Contrast. When an idea hits a person, it has to feel like something similar to an idea he or she has already experienced, yet it has to be different enough to get noticed. If every ad were the same, you wouldn't notice any (and maybe you don't). We could call Contrast differentiation, interest, or positioning. When you have Contrast right, your work strikes people as being something remarkable.

Reach. This is easy. The higher the number of people you can connect with, the more influential your idea can become. In its rawest form, Reach is about the size of your list or RSS feed, your number of followers, or how many people you connect to in other ways. The higher it is, the better. At least as far as this attribute is concerned.

Exposure. If Reach was all about how many you connect with, Exposure is all about *how often* you connect to them. Spam tries to reach you every day, yet it's likely you've never fallen prey to it. Why? We consider reaching someone more often to be better, of course, but only up to a point. Understanding Exposure will help you figure out how often, and the best ways, to connect.

Articulation. Some ideas are all over the place, and others are clear as day. High Articulation means an idea is like a sword, cutting through the fog of the brain and hitting you in exactly the right place to make you understand it. If Contrast is about being seen, Articulation is about being understood, instantly.

Trust. The subject of many books (including our 2009 best seller, *Trust Agents*), Trust still isn't entirely figured out. It's a clear factor in impact, but why do we trust someone? The answer "We feel it" simply isn't good enough. You need to know why. We'll show you.

Echo. Finally, Echo is all about the feeling of connection you give your reader, visitor, or participant. A single person could be good at Echo but could also alienate a subject entirely, while a huge corporation could, with a single swipe, make you feel something you haven't felt since childhood.

Together, these six attributes make the acronym CREATE, an easy, memorable word that is at the core of everything you'll have to do in the twenty-first-century business game. Creation is at the center of lots of your future work, and Impact is the goal. Our plan is to make it clear as day how you can do that.

This book is an opportunity that comes from a moment in

time. As you read it, you will discover that some of it is relevant to you and some of it isn't. That's okay. If you're in a small town in central Louisiana, your needs will be different from those of someone in New York City. If you're widely connected, you will have a vastly different experience from that of someone who is just starting out. This is expected. So judge from your surroundings. Figure out what parts of this opportunity work for you. Picture it like a game, and figure out the easiest, most effective moves to make. Do those first, and see what the results are. If you fail, no big deal. Keep trying. This stuff works; it's just a matter of figuring out what parts of it will work for you.

The reality is that we really are the first generation of people on this planet to be not only media consumers (like the few generations before us who listened to the radio and watched television) and media creators (which we began to be when reality television took over the airwaves). Finally, for the first time ever, we are all media owners as well. This is important, and it's the starting point for the rest of this book.

#

We think the future is bright. And we want to give you access to it. But not ten years from now. Immediately. Right now. We want to help the future along.

We want to do this by making everyone visible and helping everyone have an impact as soon as possible, by giving everyone ways to transmit their ideas as efficiently as possible, so that they can be picked up, retweeted, and remixed and have an impact on people.

Anyone can write a blog post, but not everyone can get it liked forty thousand times on Facebook, and not everyone can get seventy-five thousand blog subscribers. We've done these things, but it isn't because we're special. It's because we tried and failed, the same way you learn to ride a bike. We tried again and again, and now we have an idea how to get from point A to point B faster because of it.

In our ideal world, no idea is rejected, ignored, or forgotten because the audience is too small. In our world, people know how to convince others of the things that really matter. In our world, people know how to communicate despite the fact that society is pushing everyone to interact in person less and less. In our world, all of this comes together naturally.

In our ideal world, everyone has a chance to get heard.

So this book isn't really about the Internet at all; it's about idea and platform democracy. It's about the ability to help others with your unique ability, whatever that may be. It's about solving local and global problems more efficiently, not just for those who have monetary wealth but for those who will have the wealth of community on their side—that is to say, everyone.

We are convinced that we can do this. We are convinced that someone out there can help you find the solution to the problem you have right now. We believe that by spreading this message, we will help that person have an easier time finding you, and you them. And we believe that when you two get together, amazing things will happen. We hope you do too.

Why the Impact Equation Matters

It's important you know at least a little bit about us. We are businesspeople and media people. On the one hand, we work on projects that make us money, both online and off-line. On the other, we are media makers who use online media channels like Twitter and Google+ and blogs to build our businesses through relationships. Julien was one of the original successful podcasters, and

Chris has been a blogger for well over a decade, so we both have always used media production and digital storytelling to grow our business. This influences what we think.

The transformation we see in the media landscape is, in a sense, a power grab, and it will belong to those who are the fastest and the sharpest among us. If we've made our case properly, you should be among them, and in fact, that's where we want you to be. We want to help inform you and therefore make it easier for you to reach your people.

The next set of questions revolve not only around why and how this is important, but also around having a measurable, concrete understanding of how it works and, more importantly, when you're winning.

We're in the Wild West, so this is actually harder than it sounds. We don't truly know how the West was won, but we do know that lots of the rules from the old world got broken in an attempt to claim new territory. So we're trying here to break everything down to its essential components and nothing more. Then we take those components and try to quantify them, giving us a sense of when we're doing better or worse than the other guy. This is also kind of difficult, but that's okay; we like thinking about hard stuff.

We want to go deeper than this. We want to give you a set of metrics you can work with, something that you can bring to a team or work with by yourself to gauge how well you are doing on any given project. We want to help you figure out how to improve what you're doing by seeing what's come before. We want something you can put into an Excel spreadsheet, maybe, or even a graph.

The way we see it, any equation that helps us understand how attention and visibility work should be based not in technology but in people. After all, technology changes, but people do not. Consider this example: Imagine you are working on a campaign for your company that involves getting lots of attention to a YouTube video you've created and put online. You can measure views, retweets on Twitter, or mentions on Facebook. These are all good things. But we need more than that; we need a way to help understand how the video impacts human beings. This is not measurable by numbers alone. In 2001 David Maister, Charles Green, and Robert Galford came up with the Trust Equation, first published in the book *The Trusted Advisor*. It quantified abstract, touchy-feely concepts such as "credibility" and "intimacy" to help professionals understand their strengths and weaknesses in their professional relationships.

We've been fans of these guys for a while, so we worked with Charles Green to help quantify the phenomena we work with too. We did this because we felt that we didn't go far enough in *Trust Agents*, our last book, to help people understand how to behave on the Web. We gave people an idea of what strategies to use but no way to know when they were working. Had we done so, we would have prevented a lot of campaigns and efforts from falling flat—even our own.

By touching upon *The Trusted Advisor*'s concept of an equation in *Trust Agents*, we edged closer to what we should have done then. Like a half-completed race, we did not go far enough. Now we hope to correct that effort, leaving you with something concrete to help you gauge everything you do.

By working on each part of the equation, one at a time, you will begin to see what you're doing right, doing wrong, or not doing at all. You will see where your strengths are and why your ideas are spreading, or why they aren't spreading as much as you'd like. You'll understand what it is you need to work on, and you may even be able to prevent your mistakes.

This last part is the one that's vital. We're all for making mistakes, yes, but errors mustn't happen for their own sake (for the hell of it), but rather for learning's sake (to grow your understanding). So when you begin to use the equation, you can actually look back at your efforts, your launches, or whatever else and say, "Ah, this is what went wrong."

Here Be an Example of Brett Rogers

We introduced you to Brett Rogers earlier, discussing how he has created a career for himself as an adventurer who travels down rivers alongside other participants. The magic of his career is that he made it himself, out of a passion that he had, and that he did not need the permission of others to do it. He funded his own trips by creating adventures for others. He documented them to continue the process. As crowdfunding businesses like Kickstarter and others continue to reach the marketplace, we will see more of these, but Brett was one of the most unique, and among the first, that we saw.

But how would Brett rate on the Impact Equation? Let's use him as an example.

Contrast: Brett is like many documentary filmmakers who produce videos of their adventures. He makes us think of a few others, like Ray Zahab and Les Stroud. His category, by definition, makes him stand out, and among those in his category, he is the only one we know of who explores rivers. Beyond that, his expedition on the Mississippi led him to take some of the last footage of the Gulf of Mexico before the catastrophic BP oil spill. This further defines him and what he stands for.

Reach: Brett's Reach is relatively short by himself. He has been able to air some of his documentaries via the Documentary Channel, which extends it, but recently he's been building his audience online with a Web series called *Old Man River*. If he gets permission to communicate with that audience, his Reach will grow.

Exposure: The problem with filmmakers is that they reach people only very seldom, but the good news is that Brett is in his own films. His recent Web series will help him connect to his audience more regularly, since it is episodic. That should help his Exposure and get him remembered.

Articulation: Brett is easily defined. His story is unique and easy to retell once you've heard it: "an adventurer who travels down rivers without using a single barrel of oil." You know what it's about, and you remember it.

Trust: The style of Brett's films is raw. They are good quality while still making you feel like you are there. You see him trade jokes with his shipmates and the mistakes they make along the way. The storytelling helps you feel you know him, and reading his biography at BrettOnTheWater.com and seeing his accolades helps you trust him too.

Echo: This attribute is why we connected with Brett in the first place. His story is relatable and unique, and the emotion that he breathes into it is palpable. You can tell he cares about the rivers he travels in, that he wants to protect them and wants you to know why they matter. You watch what he does and you end up caring too.

Hey, that was easy. This is how you rate attributes of the Impact Equation. No numbers necessarily, although you can use them if you like, gauging strengths and weaknesses along the way.

RATING EACH ATTRIBUTE FOR YOURSELF

Okay, you now know the Impact Attributes and you're ready to learn about them individually. As you do this, you may discover a lot about yourself, your project, or your company. Good, that's exactly what you need to be doing. But we'd like to take this moment to show you three possible graphs, each of them rating the same project.

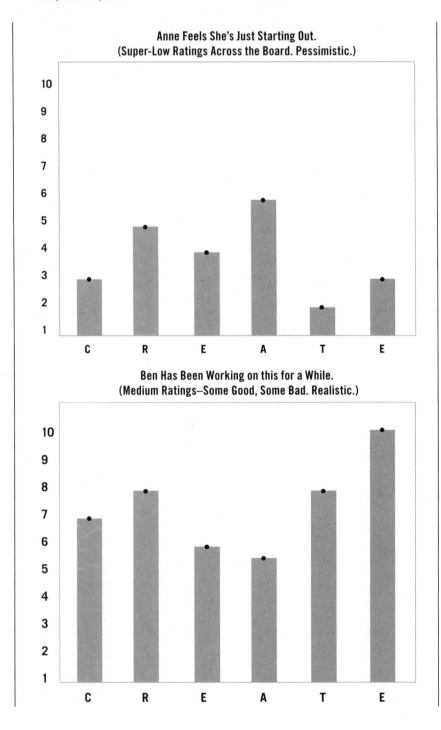

Anne Feels She's Just Starting Out.
(Super-Low Ratings Across the Board. Pessimistic.)

Ben Has Been Working on this for a While.
(Medium Ratings—Some Good, Some Bad. Realistic.)

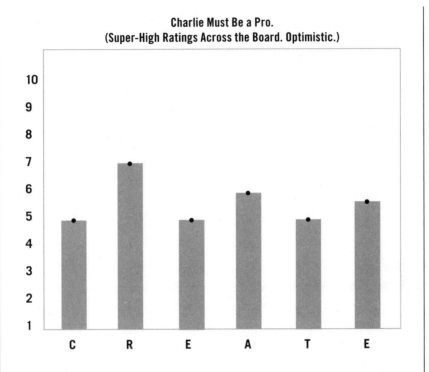

Charlie Must Be a Pro.
(Super-High Ratings Across the Board. Optimistic.)

Anne, Ben, and Charlie are all thinking about their project after reading this book. They're each wondering how they can improve what they do. Anne is having a hard time figuring out how to get a leg up on the competition. She feels her project is doing terribly, and after drawing her graph, she gets kind of depressed. Ben draws his graph and thinks, *I'm doing all right*, and Charlie thinks he's just amazing. He feels like he's batting a thousand (or close to that, anyway).

Anne, Ben, and Charlie all work on the same team, but they're each rating their project differently.

If you're Charlie, maybe you should stop patting yourself on the back so much. Start getting more ambitious. Are your sevens really huge successes? Perhaps in your industry they are. But try to set your sights higher. Divide all your ratings in two, perhaps, so you end up with something to look forward to.

Then we have Anne. Anne feels terrible because she is looking at a huge amount of work ahead of her and insurmountable odds. Those may be perfectly accurate, sure, but Anne also needs to give herself a break. It's important, when graphing the attributes, to make sure you see the differences between strong and weak areas. If everything is a one or a two, chill out. Don't hesitate to give yourself credit where credit is due.

The person who's probably getting it "right" in this example is Ben. Ben is seeing the progress that needs to be made and also the road behind himself that's been traveled. Ben has given himself room to expand and sees where his successes are. Whether he's the most objectively accurate isn't even the point. He sees where he must improve, and he sees what he has done right.

So if your graphs end up being like Charlie's or Anne's, don't give yourself the corner office or jump off the ledge just yet. Change your frame of reference and whom you're comparing yourself to, so your needs become clear. And if you still have a lot of work to do, just remember that you have plenty of time and are probably more devoted than most. After all, you bought this book, didn't you?

\#

There's more to think about here than just the attributes. The attributes themselves are also divided into four sections that will give you a general set of guiding principles to develop the work you do in the right direction. Here they are.

Goals: When we think about it, it's kind of amazing how many people operate in the world without a clear and definite goal. The first time we asked entrepreneur Gary Vaynerchuk about his goals, he said, "Buy the Jets," before we'd even finished asking the question. There was no pause, no hesitation. Building useful goals and working aggressively toward accomplishing them is a trait we assumed was common, but we've found it could use a bit of shoring up for most people. Some people have goals but can't communicate them by creating ideas. Or they move on from day to day through the usual corridor of decisions without really considering where it will lead them. This is a natural thing for people to do, but it's not an effective way to achieve something great.

Ideas: Both of us run into many people who have developed a decent Reach via their efforts to form a platform but haven't decided what they stand for or what that platform can do that would be useful and valuable to others. In some cases, it is a matter of someone not really spending enough time on their goals. In other cases, it was simply that the person couldn't articulate their ideas clearly or make them stand out. It's been said that everything has two births: first as an idea and then as the real and tangible output of that idea. But the idea and the output won't matter if people don't know about them or believe they matter.

Platform: What we didn't write enough about in *Trust Agents* was the concept of having a platform, this sense that it takes more than a steady stream of tweets or blog posts to build a voice that will have Impact. Maybe it's because we were doing this kind of thing naturally or because we incorrectly presumed that "everyone" knew how to build up a platform. A platform is a way to extend your voice beyond the ears closest to you. It might be something mainstream, like appearing on a television show or having articles published in newspapers or magazines, or more often, it might be a creative use of one or more social-networking tools, used with intent and across many platforms.

Human Element: This was (is!) perhaps the bread and butter of *Trust Agents*. The premise was that most people were using the Web in ways that were skipping the human element of business. Relationship-minded practices weren't translating well. With social networks and social media, there was a new potential for fixing this. But since *Trust Agents*, we still see many people skip the relationship and community aspects of online business (and sometimes off-line as well). There is still much to say to help people communicate and do business with as much impact as possible.

So the remaining sections of the book will focus on ideas, platform, and the human element. We'll use the rest of this chapter to talk about goals, why they matter, learning how to set them, etc. But before we continue this, we'd like to clear up one final point.

The impact you leave on your customers, potential customers, and ex-customers is the business inside your business. When the impact is both positive and big, your ideas can spread on their own. Even ex-customers may talk about you because you have done something different, if you do it right. So while not as important as, you know, keeping your business afloat, the impact of your business is significant.

And inside the impact of your business, it has become our sincere belief that unless you are working on improving one or many of our sections—ideas, platform, or the human element—you are simply doing it wrong. Let's explain.

Refining your ideas is a key part of the equation. So is building a platform and working on the human aspect. At any time, if you are wondering what you should be doing with your work or how you should be improving it, our general answer is that only these three aspects of marketing matter in the world of media. They are everything and they will direct you toward what you should work on.

Recently Julien met an incredibly smart guy, a professor at the John Molson School of Business named Gad Saad. The guy is straight-up brilliant. He invented evolutionary psychology as it relates to consumption. This means that he knows why you bought the Acura instead of the Honda with the same features, even though it cost twenty-five thousand dollars more.

You've probably met someone like this: brilliant, witty, a nice guy, well respected in his field, etc. Yet Julien couldn't help but ask himself: *Why is this guy not world famous?* You could dismiss it as luck, but we don't think that's the answer at all. What's really going on is that Professor Saad has no platform.

He has every other part of the equation down pat. He has smart ideas, invented a whole field, and differentiated himself with it. He knows how to speak in front of others, etc. But he simply doesn't have a wide enough launchpad from which to transmit his own ideas, so he's dependent on the platforms of others. This is a weakness. And when you know this, you realize that the primary thing Gad should be working on is his platform, because it will drastically impact his results.

The same thing is true of people who have wide platforms and great ideas but are considered to be egotistical and selfish. They are not good with people, so despite their success at reaching tons of people, having great ideas to talk about, maybe even selling tons of books, seminars, etc., the reality is that no one wants to work with them. These people are simply not nice, so organizations work with them only reluctantly. Their human element is missing because they don't care, so they flounder when they should thrive.

Finally, there are some who have huge platforms and are great people. They know how to connect very widely, remember everyone's name, and may have hundreds of thousands of Twitter followers or more. Their work naturally gets sent out more than others, and they get tons of attention. Yet a lack of really interesting ideas prevents them from reaching the next level.

Let's say you're feeling overwhelmed. There are too many things to do. The economy has left you with fewer people to share the burden and you're fighting over smaller scraps. Customers aren't as easy to satisfy as they used to be. They most definitely aren't as loyal. And bills at home are going up and up. You're not seeing any real end to the way things seem to be, and you're not nearly as clear on what has to happen next to sustain yourself. So your goals might be:

1. Embrace the chaos. Understanding that nothing will ever revert to the way it was before, start thinking that way. Build everything you do on acceptance that things will permanently be changing. This goal might make you more comfortable with accepting that "job security" is a myth. You might realize that you need more money in the bank for more pivots.

2. Romance thirty. This is a business goal. You want to treat your thirty best customers (or whatever number you think you can manage) very well. You want to pay very close attention to their needs. You want to give them concierge-class service every day. You want to know much more about them than about any other buyers who come and go in your business.

3. Move. Fitness and health might matter to you. Before you sign on to the idea of spending even more time in front of your computer, think about how you are going to blend in your fitness goals. What will you do to ensure that your day has a cadence and rhythm that include movement? Again, we're just making these stories up, but maybe they resonate with you.

4. Stay lean. Again, a business goal. You might choose to keep features and services to a minimum around your offerings. You might cut the projects that aren't pulling enough weight. If you're an employee at the mercy of others, maybe this means understanding how to prioritize, or maybe it means some internal campaigning to understand what you can convince the leadership you might drop.

You see how this works? Every "goal" is a guidepost. It's a way to make decisions. It's a flag to march toward. That's how we think about goals. This isn't "Lose twenty pounds by April 30 by cutting out sweets and eating more salads." It's looking at the bigger picture to drive tactical daily changes.

In this case, understanding your goals clearly helps with Contrast, Articulation, and to some extent Trust and Echo, and in other cases it'll align with other Impact Attributes. Aligning the rest of your efforts around building Impact and the core of your goals is the only way you'll succeed in making ideas, platform, and the human element work in delivering what you want.

Just being there isn't enough anymore.

The Attention War

One of the main differences between the channels we used to have and the ones being built now is that the ones we used to have were very expensive. Having a television or radio station, putting together a BBS, printing a newspaper—all of these things required technical expertise, lots of money, or both.

Things aren't like this anymore. Getting a radio station was expensive, but now we have stations that cost nothing to make, like Twitter feeds, that are supported by companies' infrastructures and given to you at no cost. And because it costs nothing to create these channels, they are also cheap to maintain. All they require is your time.

This is a fundamental change in the way culture is unfolding in our age. Anyone can choose to be an owner, if they like. The costs of upkeep are almost zero. The time you spend is largely in creation of content instead of in traditional areas like investing, hiring, and distribution.

Consider how this changes things. Being a media mogul (in the traditional sense of the phrase) means being rich, which also usually means being pretty old, middle-aged at the very least. All of the empires of our age, all of the skyscrapers and cities, were built by these people, usually older white men with great vision who wanted to forge something in their image. America, Canada, and almost everywhere else was made that way—paid for by industry and media. All the towers in our cities say so: Bank of America, CBS, Goldman Sachs, they're all there.

Something is different now. On the Web, thirteen-year-olds can become millionaires faster than their fathers could have earned a tenth that much. These aren't just anomalies either; they're our largest success stories. Zuckerberg, Brin, Page—all of them began by leveraging tools that didn't require a massive inheritance or tens of thousands of employees. When young people can have an influence so large, both through wealth and through their companies, the culture itself has to change.

But this transformation doesn't apply just to them; it applies to everyone. The tools they used are available to everyone, for free—and even if you don't use them to become the next Henry Ford of your era, they can at least make a better life for you and those who come after you.

That is why this is important. A long time ago, the industrialists saw their Reach increasing and took advantage of it. They became heroes of their time, but many others saw this change as well, did nothing, and became no one. No one talks about them. They did not change the world for the better; they just thought about it.

The reality is that this transformation in media is happening. It's happening now, and it is a moment in time that will never repeat itself—not in the same way it's happening now. If you are among the first to know how to leverage it, you can go places and have advantages you never could have imagined before.

But in order to be there, most people must be deprogrammed a little. You must stop thinking in the factory mind-set, the method all of us learned, and start thinking like a magnate. You must start thinking as if you were someone who has just inherited a great thing, a precious resource that will not last forever but can bring greatness. Because, in a way, you have. You have a chance to own something that no person in your family has ever had—great visibility, huge Reach, massive access, and maybe some extra cash to go along with them.

But this requires you to stop thinking like an employee. No one here will tell you what to do, because no one wants you to take anything away from them. An employee, by definition, makes money for other people—it must be the case, or he wouldn't get hired in the first place. The owner, on the other hand, creates value for himself and his family. So whether you are creating value by building a sense of freedom, learning how to do more with less, or creating more income, the mind-set is the same: Think like an owner.

Owners, for example, search out opportunities, while employees wait for opportunities to come to them. Owners create their own job titles by creating their own jobs, while employees wait for job openings to exist before they rise—which is a form of asking for permission.

There will be a time when everyone will think this way. Everyone will know that they are in control because no one else will really take care of them. The set paths will have failed—one could argue, for example, that "higher learning" will no longer be a direction that makes sense for most people, leaving many people unsure as to where their next move will be. What to do will no longer be obvious. People will have to take control in order to get anything done at all.

But that time hasn't come yet, which contributes to its importance. Having knowledge that other people don't is profitable, and if you are reading this, you will learn more about how to spread your ideas, how to build your platform, and how to communicate than almost anyone. This is a huge asset. We hope you get as much out of it as we have.

But let's be clear: All this mind-set talk isn't some self-help nonsense. It isn't about "think and make it happen"; it's just about seeing an opportunity that is more accessible now than ever before. This is about a moment in time when some advantages are easier to obtain than others. So this book is simply a guide to making sure you don't waste the advantages you have. That is all.

Thinking about channels so far in this book has been mostly about communication, but realize that there are more ways to look at this concept. Distribution is another element of a channel. Building on what we've already covered here, realize this:

- Zappos sells shoes via the Web, which was originally considered to be a crazy idea no one, customers or investors, would ever buy in to. (It sells much more than shoes now.)

- Chris bought his Camaro via the Web, with only a few photos and the help of a seller who runs a virtual-only car dealership.

- Platforms like Google+ are empowering paid private tutoring and coaching of small groups, augmenting a practice that was once limited to working with people in a specific geography.

■ Publishing in any digital format is free (or ridiculously close to it). You need no one's permission to post material in text, audio, photo, video, or other formats. Distribution is equally free (to people with Internet access).

The frictionless nature of all this bears considering when we talk about the expenses of a channel. We have the power to reduce the friction of communication *and* the previous friction of distribution infrastructure to unprecedented price points (often free).

Since we are talking about goals, it's important to understand that a channel being free or inexpensive monetarily doesn't mean it's without other costs. To maintain this kind of channel, as we've pointed out, takes a lot of time and creative effort, plus a lot of nurturing. This requires that you consider your options before choosing to take action.

We Are All Fledgling TV Stations

We believe the path to achieving impact is to drive the CREATE formula of the Impact Equation through goals, into ideas, and onto a well-developed platform and then to follow up by nurturing the human elements of your community. We're implicitly advocating that you accept your new role as a media creator, whether or not this has anything to do with your primary purpose.

Julien summed it up well by saying that we are perhaps the first generation who are not only mass consumers of media in multiple formats but also mass creators of media.

What if you (or your business) were a TV station? You have a channel. You must now curate information and content that is informative, useful, and promotes return visits. If this didn't instantly bring a shiver to you, we're surprised. It seems like a lot to comprehend. It seems like a lot of work. It seems like there must be easier ways to build influence and create impact. Strike "easier" from your repertoire. Nothing worth doing is easy. Simple, sometimes. Easy? Never.

But this really is worth considering. If you want to reach people, and if you want to stand out and bring ideas to a platform that then takes an action, thinking of yourself as a TV station is a good starting point. Think of the responsibility. If you are programming the "Portland Real Estate TV" network, what does that look like?

Most businesses approach this challenge by creating only autobiographical content. What is an advertisement if not a piece of information that tells your audience all about you? There's nothing wrong with advertisements, but would *you* tune in to a TV station that talked all about one company or one person or one product all day long?

We tune in to passions. If you are a golf lover, you'll watch the golf station for quite some time and feel like it's time well spent. But each show is different. Each show is another element or aspect of this passionate ecosystem. Some shows will teach you how to perfect your swing or your grip (neither of us plays golf, so we're winging it a bit). Others will interview current professional players. Some shows will be about the technology. Other shows might cover the business around the sport. If you stopped what you were doing right now and wrote down ten discrete "shows" to put on a golf channel, you'd probably be able to do that.

Now do it for your own pursuits.

Where most people go wrong is that they say, "I'm multifaceted. I can't limit myself to one passion." Very few people *aren't* multifaceted. That's why your TV has a remote control and why there are many channels. However, your goal is to focus your ideas into one larger story line wherein your "shows" will have something thematic in common.

The USA Network's tagline is "Characters welcome." It's built the theme of its station around the idea that interesting characters are what drives its programming choices. Bravo is built around reality shows (a mix of trashy ones and educational ones). Other networks are actually a lot harder to pin down, and interestingly, when we checked the ratings for those networks, they're not doing as well. It seems that the modern method of programming television is to keep your theme reasonably focused.

You *can* find a theme that encompasses all you want to cover, if you view your effort to build a platform and share ideas as similar to building a TV station. And the goal should be to make that theme broad enough to cover all your interests in some form or another (or some larger set of your interests) while still keeping a focus or themed element.

When we say "TV station," realize that the world has changed. It's not like we mean that you're creating video to fill twenty-four hours. We mean that you're going to create whatever content you intend to create and distribute it across whatever elements of your platform you can develop. This might mean e-mail newsletters, blog posts, video content, tweets, and more.

Take a few moments and think about this. Don't rush to the next segment. Pause and ask yourself what the TV station of you (or your business, or both!) looks like. Ask yourself whom it serves. Ask whether you can think of even ten story ideas that match thematically. Brainstorm just a bit. Let your right-brain juices flow on the next page, which we have intentionally left blank.

Why This Book Isn't About Facebook

Okay, so congratulations, you now have a Twitter account. Unfortunately, we don't care.

Maybe you have a blog too. We don't care about that either. In fact, we don't give a damn that you have a Twitter, a Facebook, a blog, or a Google+. We don't care that you have a Foursquare, a Groupon, or a whatever the hell else you're going to have next.

Congratulations, you now have the newest gadget the tech world has ever seen. Still, nobody cares. Even you, the owner, might not even care.

You are not on our radar. You are not on our map. There is a big blank space where your name should be in the dictionary, and even if it were there, nobody would look it up. Nobody knows your name or has a reason to look for you, or even if they do, it doesn't matter, because you're boring.

Yet we are in an age replete with stories of average guys and girls who have achieved massive success online even though they were regular schmucks. They fell into it. Their career biographies mirror the lives of the Olsen twins—they were just magically discovered one day and became famous. No serious work was done, and no suffering or sacrifice occurred. It just happened.

The problem, such as it is, is that everyone has a whatever account. Everyone is using social media. At the time of this writing, over eight hundred million people use Facebook. That's more than one in eleven humans on the planet. So just being there isn't enough. If you build it, they won't come. Definitely not right away, but in this day and age, possibly never.

But even though we started this segment with a discouraging tone, all is not lost. All we want to point out is that it will take more than "being there" to deliver impact. What comes next is determining how to deliver information that's useful to the people you hope to reach and how to build relationships that lead to value.

That should be your goal for using these new channels. If you're interested in social-media software, don't pick it up because it's free or because "it's what the kids are using." Time isn't free, and the largest segment of people getting involved in social networks are people between the ages of thirty and sixty, so they're big kids.

The goal, instead, is to use these simple, low-friction technologies to reach people with similar interests. Logging in to Google+ and searching for people who want what you're selling is a very good use of your time. Logging in to post pictures of your products and waiting for the cash register to ring might not work as well.

Oh, and you have to be there with your ears as much as your mouth. Just shouting into these new channels isn't effective. You'll get some attention, but it's limited. The real value comes when you listen to what others are saying and learn to comment in ways that embrace these new interactions, not simply sell your product. Yes, you can sell, but it's a little deeper into the cycle.

We'll paraphrase Clay Shirky: Now that the tools have become *technologically* boring, they can become *socially* interesting. The tools aren't cool because they're new tools. They're cool because they let you interact in new ways. Your first cell phone was cool for a few weeks, and then it was a tool that let you check with your spouse about whether or not there was enough milk for morning cereal. That same tool allows you to open deals and/or warm up prospects. Welcome to the new tools, same as the old. Only better, because you actually know what to do with them. It's almost like puberty all over again.

Leveling Up

When you start out in any video game, you start at level one. You have the fewest tools, the fewest abilities, the fewest resources. No matter which game you play, the mechanics are that you learn new skills along the way, you acquire new tools, and your experience prepares you for more complicated and involved challenges. But there's this little, less discussed aspect of all this.

In almost every game with a narrative, there are ways to run around and acquire more resources and experience by doing busy-work. (Pac-Man doesn't exactly have this concept, but World of Warcraft does.) For instance, in the console game Skylanders (which is a lot of fun, even for grown-ups!), your characters gain abilities by earning experience points, which come from defeating foes. You can, should you wish, keep fighting smallish, low-power foes and thus slowly gain experience that still helps you meet your needs. You can also try to collect every piece of treasure along the way, to buy upgrades for your characters.

This is usually the less fulfilling way to get to another level, but in many of these games, you have to get there somehow, and that's one way to do it. You either do the grind of swatting little monsters and collecting every scrap of gold you can or you risk your character's progress at every step of the game. Sounds like life, doesn't it? (Related but not, there's a great fiction-but-really-close-to-real-life-happenings book by Cory Doctorow called *For the Win* that covers some fascinating aspects of this.)

A Mix of Two Strategies

There's grunt work required. You have to collect the gold and swat the little monsters every now and again, even if it's boring and un-fulfilling. In the "real" world, this means doing the grunt work at your job. It means filing your bills on time. It means practicing the day-to-day stuff that brings you success. That's what we talked about above.

But then, the good stuff happens when you leverage your practice and grunt work into calculated leaps. Smallish leaps at first, but we're talking about taking what you've learned, extrapolating, and then taking a big swing at something that gets you there while bypassing some of the grunt levels.

If you're feeling a little bit of "Whoa, this is way too much video-game chat there, cowboys. I don't even play solitaire on my computer," let us break it down with no video-game analogies for a moment. (Then we'll switch back.)

Two Ways to Achieve Your Goals

1. Do the daily work and practice those tasks and skills that sustain your baseline.

2. Make (semicalculated) bigger moves toward goals you can't easily attain.

Julien walked eight hundred kilometers in one big go (a massive and legendary pilgrimage). That's not something you just do one day. But it's also bigger than walking or running a few miles every day, which is necessary to build the baseline. Almost everything Chris does follows this pattern: Do the groundwork and then take big swings. Be willing to recorrect and adjust, and hold the goal and the practice together in the same loose handhold.

Writing a book is like that. Both of us are bloggers. We're good at getting a handful of words down into a post. But a book is not a series of blog posts (much to the grief of several book editors who have to deal with books that feel like a bunch of blog posts).

A book is, one hopes, a cohesive big idea spread out into enough information to let you grasp the concepts and then make them your own. But this doesn't just happen on its own. It takes a lot of concerted effort in both areas above: grinding out the time on the keyboard and taking wild swings at bigger goals/ideas.

Back to Leveling Up

As we write this, the video-game culture has silently (not really) shot past the U.S. movie culture in terms of revenue. Think about this: People take days off of work to play the latest version of Madden NFL or Call of Duty. No one sneaks out of work to watch a movie. And if they do, that's two hours, versus entire weeks taken off to push through games like Skyrim.

Study after study has shown that those who play video games have previously unnoticed skills that map wonderfully to business pursuits. Heck, look at the U.S. military. Predator pilots are playing the ultimate video game. (Okay, some of you might cringe at thinking of it that way. Yes, we realize that war is deadly and real. *Technically*, they are wobbling some joysticks and playing a remote experience digitally. It's not a *game* but it's a similar experience.)

Books like *Reality Is Broken* by Jane McGonigal, *Game On* by Jon Radoff, and several more point out how game culture is creeping into business culture and then some. You don't have to take our word for it. But what to do with this as it applies to your goals and impact?

ACTION: GET YOUR GAME FACE ON

Want to start thinking about leveling up and games? What most real-world systems are missing is any kind of meaningful scoring and feedback system (among other traits). For instance, most employees get an annual review. Do you really have to wait a year to know how you're doing? A month is probably too long, right? Make your own metrics.

We'll talk about it throughout the book in different ways, but it's important to realize this: Your path is your path, and that has nothing to do with your current "job." It has everything to do with your goals. So get your game face on.

1. Pick a metric for everything you're doing that matters. If you want to be a better marketer, make your metric the number of subscribers on your e-mail list (or whatever). If you want to be healthy, pick a metric like "consecutive days of thirty minutes or more of activity." Simple. Pick simple metrics. Where *everyone* goes wrong in this is in looking for too many numbers.

2. Level up. If your goal is to earn a million dollars next year, break that into monthly revenue (around $84,000) and make your daily grind include something to move that number. Even if you get to 10 percent of that by year-end, you're doing great.

3. Take a wild swing. This is variable. It might mean seeking an introduction to someone above your "pay grade." It might mean applying for a job you're not qualified for. Try something bigger than what should be next in a natural progression. There's risk, but the rewards are big too.

4. Play new games. Once you're feeling fairly comfortable with the game you're playing, look for a new way to mix it up. A few years back, Julien took on MovNat and CrossFit and many other fitness challenges

to see just what he was capable of accomplishing. As we're writing this book, Chris is relaunching his music studies for a project with Jacqueline Carly about blending ancient Indian chanting music with modern digital effects and tools. The moment you get too eased into the game you're playing is the moment you'll miss the chance to level up.

Actors and Spectators

The first definition of an actor is the one you think of when you hear the word: someone who performs in a play or movie or dramatization. The word comes from a Greek word meaning "to interpret." The second definition is a lot less sexy to most people: a person who does something; a participant. That's the one we find sexy. There's a huge difference between actors and spectators, and if you want your ideas to have impact, you have to be a participant.

Every activity or pursuit has its own little industry. For every professional basketball player on the court, there are people paid to hand out hot dogs, people paid to sweep up after everyone has gone home, people paid to write about the game, people paid to train those players, and so on. In their own little way, every one of those people is an actor.

If you're watching the game, either at home or from the stands, you're a spectator. Thank you for your money. That earns you the privilege of being in the arena (provided you don't angrily throw your beer on someone else). If you're home, you pay by loaning your eyeballs to a TV channel that sells ads against the likelihood of your being there to watch (and maybe you pay the cable TV company, if that's what it requires to gain access to a televised game). But you're still a spectator.

In many pursuits, there are spectators who believe (for whatever reason) that they too are actors. There are many people who feel that their love of watching movies should pay their bills. This is only exacerbated by people like Harry Knowles, who started a site to review films, who then wrote lots of negative reviews of an early screening of *Batman & Robin* (and as a Batman fan, Chris concurs that this movie deserves every angry review), and whom studio execs blamed for the movie's poor performance (instead of blaming the fact that the Bat-people's costumes had nipples and George Clooney gave one of his only clunker performances ever, and . . . well, we have to stop now).

For every Harry who makes it, there are thousands of people who believe they will succeed by being a spectator and won't. One of the first and most important dividers determining whether or not your ideas will have impact is whether they are the ideas of an actor or a spectator. This isn't for us to decide. And by the way, we are always both. The point is, if the idea you're looking to move through the Impact Equation is to be successful, it should be the idea of an actor.

It's Okay to Be a Spectator . . . Sometimes

You're not meant to be an actor in everything. To do so is to risk never mastering what it takes to succeed in those areas or pursuits that might best nourish you. We are all spectators. We like music but might never be in a "real" band. We love movies but probably won't end up in a major motion picture (maybe Julien will). We've held jobs (Chris more than Julien) where the role handed to us was more a spectator's role. But once you decide to be the actor on an idea of your own creation, then the rocket ship takes off.

Never presume for a moment that being an actor is some kind of trumpet call that comes from others. And once you decide to be an actor on some idea in your life, it's not like the world gets suddenly easier. In fact, it often gets more difficult.

Actors Are Not Universally Hailed

Chris wrote a somewhat controversial cover article for *Success* magazine about celebrity marketing, of which the lion's share was about Kim Kardashian. If you have no idea who that is, either you're to be celebrated or you might be visiting from another planet. She is best known for a popular reality TV show but also manages several product lines and several endorsement packages and produced a reality TV show around a New York–based PR firm.

Readers and commenters complained that they didn't feel Kardashian was the model of success they had come to associate with the magazine of the same name. However, reading more deeply into many of the comments and letters, what came up over and over were complaints that she had a famous stepfather or that she got a boost from having a sex tape. (Fancy that: She's only famous because someone released a sex tape about her? Seems that would be detrimental to one's success, not a win.) If she didn't have a reality show, some said, she wouldn't be successful.

Everyone who chooses to launch ideas, build a platform, and navigate the human element will be met with criticism. Everyone who dares to "come up" from their beginnings will be challenged. Musician and businessman 50 Cent has said several times that many of the people who supported him when he first started in music were the same ones who said he was "getting too big for his britches" when he was invited to record his first mainstream album.

Actors Have Just as Many Excuses as You, Maybe More

Ryan Blair was a gang member with a horrible family life. He learned how to build a business, hit some bumps along the way, and is now a very successful multimillionaire. Sir Richard Branson has dyslexia. He's doing okay, we hear. Glenda Watson Hyatt has very limited use of her motor skills and is difficult to understand when you speak with her. She wrote an entire book with her left thumb and continues to write long and meaty posts at her blog (doitmyselfblog.com) quite frequently. Julien has hearing problems as well as epilepsy. Chris has severe clinical depression.

We all have excuses. There are obstacles in everyone's way. But if you're going to make your ideas happen and learn about impact, you're going to have to accept your excuses and flaws and obstacles and do it anyway. That's that dividing line we talked about earlier. Actors don't let excuses get in the way. And again, we don't mean Hollywood actors. We mean participants. We mean you.

Build Before the Need

So you may not know why you need a platform right now. You may not realize why a channel is important not just for those on a mission—those who run a business or have a cause—but for everyone. You may think, *I have a normal life. I don't have a message to spread. I don't have any new ideas. Why should I take part in this?*

If this is where you're coming from, we get it. Not everyone feels the need to shoot their mouth off on the Internet, as we do. Understandable. But developing a channel is about more than expression. It's about strategy, and it's an important step for your personal life, your business, and your career. It's something you need to be doing not when you are working on your new project, but much earlier than that. Otherwise, it will be too late.

Imagine you move to a new town and you need a job. You go from place to place, from general store to barbershop to drive-in movie theater (this is clearly an old-fashioned town). You visit everyone and tell them your story. It is possible to get a job if you tell your story well; after all, if you're a good salesman, you can sell yourself. But many people aren't, and they come to the end of Main Street and realize they still haven't found anything. No previous connection with these people means no one has any reason to trust you with their shop.

Now imagine the opposite happens. You still need a job, but you're in your hometown, and everyone knows you. You have a history with them. Your network is strong in this place, and as you go down Main Street, you know everyone. Now ask yourself how long it will take before you are offered work. It will be much quicker. Even if people don't know you, they may know your parents or your grandparents. There is a history, and with those bonds come many more opportunities.

Think of your neighbor. You don't befriend him because you'll need a cup of milk. You do it because it's a good thing to do, and it's good to know your neighbors.

The same thinking should apply to your network and your need to create a channel. You may not know why you need to do this, since you have no cause to support, no idea to spread, or anything else. But when you do have such an idea or something that needs attention, wouldn't you rather know your entire neighborhood? Wouldn't you rather spread it to two hundred people than to, say, ten?

But getting your list to two hundred isn't as easy as it looks, and it certainly doesn't happen instantly. This is why starting early is so important, just as we're always told to begin saving early for retirement, even though nobody actually does. The earlier something begins, the more powerful it is, even if it begins only with friends and family and moves up from there.

The first few members of your network are hard to build, and it's a big challenge at first, but the audience builds more easily over time. So doing the hard part early, as in any endeavor, is important. Starting now is key.

Channels that start now have other advantages as well. Just as in writing, the more practice you get, the easier it becomes, and getting that practice early, while no one is paying attention, is valuable because there is little downside to writing badly for an audience of no one. As you get better at your craft, the audience will grow, and by the time it's significant, you'll be much better.

So the message is actually simple: Do the hard part now in order to reap the rewards later. This message will be repeated again and again throughout this book, because it relates directly to all three parts of visibility: idea, platform, and human element, which all need work before they can become significant assets, sometimes for quite a long time.

Over time, as you progress with these ideas, you will also make them your own, so your model of how to create content, or build platform, etc., will develop into something that is uniquely yours. But as you're doing it, you must never act as if you had made it— that is to say, as if you had already gone far enough. You need to act as you did the first day, as if you had nothing.

Acting as if you had no audience will help you work harder than most people around you. You will be less defensive about what you own and naturally work to build more instead of being afraid to lose what you have.

But however you continue to build audience, you must begin before the need. It's like your walk down Main Street; don't begin when you're broke. Begin when you're doing well and don't need anything at all. The results will be better, and when your time of need comes, it'll seem significantly less needy.

As goals go, building before the need is an important one. It means that you recognize the importance and value of attention, and nurturing this platform will allow you to share ideas that can then take shape into something of further value.

It's not easy to keep people's attention. It's not easy to build something like this without having even a vague sense of the potential audience you want to gather around you. Here are some thoughts about what might work for you.

■ Tell stories about the people in your community. Even when your community in this new channel is fewer than fifty people, you can talk about the people who are there. Do it early. Do it often. People want to see themselves, want to identify, want to belong. Business is about belonging.

■ Be helpful. The more you can share *how* to do things that matter to your community, the more likely they'll come back for more. People interpret the world through a "what's in it for me" lens, no matter how saintly they ultimately act.

■ Be personable. The more human you are in connecting with this channel, the more it will benefit you later on. Every piece of information you share is a great representation of your company's value. When you talk about how your grandfather used to take you fishing and how that changed the way you approach problems, that will be remembered long after the details of your business story.

■ Be concise. Don't waste people's time. In developing and building a channel before it's needed, flooding and overwhelming people isn't helpful. In this world of mobile-device domination and excessive drains on our time, people want to consume bite-size chunks of information. It's tapas, not a buffet. Make sure to share in brief formats as often as possible. (See this bulleted list? We rest our case.)

■ Share value. Use your channel to help connect your community with value. For instance, if you introduce two people from your community and they're able to do business (without your asking for anything in the transaction), that kind of effort gets remembered. In *Trust Agents*, we called this being at the elbow of every deal.

■ Be original. As often as possible, share unique perspectives, ideas, and information that come from far outside the typical source material for your community. If you're selling fishing gear, don't repost articles you find in *American Angler* magazine. Everyone in your community already read that story when you did. Instead, look for stories that are interesting and helpful but that come from far outside the normal channels. It's easier than you think. (Google helps.)

It doesn't cost a lot of money to develop this kind of channel. Thankfully, these days, it isn't about money. It's about how much you're willing to work.

#

But what to work on? The Web is huge, and there are so many different types of companies out there. You're probably thinking, *I have a ton of ideas, I could execute on any of them* or maybe *I have no idea what I should create. I wouldn't even know where to begin!*

Well, no matter what your stance, it's the process of starting that matters. Starting once, on any given day, is easy. Starting every single day is hard, but it's how your media will be created, how your book will get written, and how your empire will be built. As Kimon Nicolaides once said, "There is no such thing as getting more than you put into anything." In other words, the work creates the results. There are no shortcuts.

It's in this vein that we introduce, in the next section, the laboratory in which you should develop, refine, and sharpen your ideas. Execution is everything, this is true, but before something is released to the world it needs to be considered, experimented with, and properly polished. It needs to be handled and designed until it has the best shape, so when it's sent into the world, it can be properly caught by your audience. But more important, your brain needs to be able to wrap itself around what a good idea even *is* in the first place. You may think you can recognize a good, spreadable idea when you see one. If this is true, congratulations are in order, because there are few who really can.

We intend to put that knowledge into the hands of everyone. So if you want to learn, read on.

PART 2 Ideas

Attending the South by Southwest conference in Austin, Texas, is a little like visiting the future.

It starts slowly. The plane lands, and your iPhone suddenly tells you that ten or twenty of your friends are at the airport at the exact same time you are. You arrive at the center of town, where you can use Wi-Fi absolutely everywhere (last year, in a controversial move, a company paid homeless people to walk around as mobile hot spots). You pay for taxis by liking them on Facebook, and sometimes the hotel upgrades you based on how many Twitter followers you have. You also know which restaurant all of your acquaintances are visiting tonight, and you detect the location of every party around through your phone.

This is just a taste of what happens during the weeklong festival, a kind of Mecca for indie types, including many Web personalities and their fans. It's amazing how crowded the space, and your brain, becomes.

South by Southwest is a place where everyone understands where the Web is going. They all download the newest apps. They all move at the speed of Silicon Valley, not the speed of the rest of the world. So visiting it truly is like attending a party in the future, where everyone has a blog or a Web app they're trying to tell you about. Everyone is launching a new game or a new service they want you to try. They're funded by important venture capitalists, and they believe in what they're doing. Unfortunately, the truth is, not all of them can win.

More quickly than you can imagine, you become immune to this bombardment of information and hype. It hits the retina and dies there before entering the brain. You begin to build a kind of mental and emotional fortress, as you would if you were walking through a village torn apart by war.

You have no choice. You can't arrive and listen to everything. You get skeptical. You stop listening to anyone who seems too interested. Even attendees from small towns, who are used to saying hi to strangers on the street, become suddenly aloof.

This place is a kind of physical manifestation of the marketplace of ideas you travel through every day if you use the Web at all. Visiting it in a physical place is different, and most are unused to the feeling it evokes—a sense of ignoring a lot of the wildness that is going on, as if you were visiting a mining town in the Old West where everyone is trying to sell you something, or a bazaar in which you are being cajoled into stall after stall, or maybe even a carnival where barkers call out to you. Everyone wants a piece. They're hungry for your attention, because the more of it they get, the brighter their own future becomes.

The only thing that keeps the Web from feeling like this on a daily basis is the filters that have been placed at the walls of your city, preventing most ideas from hitting you at all. You only see things that your friends post or that have been voted to the top of Reddit.com, so you aren't exposed to every single thing the way you are in Austin during that week. So your Web experience is calmer and less defensive. You can have more faith in the things that you see, because they have been filtered. But in the real world, there are people in your physical space. Ignoring them is difficult. You begin to get a real idea of just how crowded this carnival is.

But seeing this conference in person means you can begin to understand what the marketplace of ideas is really about. You can grasp just how many ideas are out there, wanting your attention. You can experience people's truly bad ideas instead of filtering them out at the gates. The hordes are visible and accessible. You can choose what to pay attention to, that is, if you can make sense of the chaos at all.

As you imagine this scene (or remember it, if you've been), realize that it's how the future will look. If you live in New York, it may happen more quickly. If you live in South Dakota, perhaps a little more slowly. But as time goes on, as it becomes less expensive to produce and distribute content, you will be exposed to more ideas more often, and you will get better at choosing among them. In other words, you will become more discerning. The quality of ideas will have to keep up with your galvanized mental barriers.

That's right, you and the rest of the audience, just as in a bazaar, will become even more cynical and discerning than you are now. It will be harder to impress audiences tomorrow than today, as it is harder today than yesterday.

So you must begin as soon as possible. You must realize that your ideas, almost all of them, are simply not strong enough to survive in the modern idea ecosystem. They haven't evolved enough. They haven't encountered enough challenges. You haven't worked on distilling them enough or sharpening them like a sword. They cannot cut through the armor that shields your potential audience's minds.

This will be the first step in understanding how impact works. The more complex and competitive the ecosystem, the more adaptable and targeted your messages must become.

Forget the things you've heard, the myths like "good content markets itself." It may have been true once, but it isn't anymore. Yes, the strongest ideas survive, but content creators are getting more savvy every day. They know what you like, and they are designing their work around it. They are curating the experience to make sure every part is delightful, and unless you can compete with that, your work will be forgotten.

Ideas are not organic things that are simply born out of a brain, fully formed. They are crafted the way writers craft sentences and stories. They are edited over and over again and go from lumps of clay to masterpieces. But most people are never in the idea laboratory, so they don't see this process. For example, imagine the difference between this manuscript when it was created and the final state in which you are reading it today. How much better is it? Would you have read it in its original, unpolished form?

This also means that most people cannot throw out one idea a year and expect to succeed. They must be consistent in their experimentation in order to understand what the marketplace wants. Everyone has to get better at designing and polishing. Only this kind of labor will allow you to truly understand how an idea survives.

Thankfully, there is a system behind all this that almost everyone on the Web understands to some degree. Some get it instinctively; others have learned over time. We'd like to help you skip the line and teach you what we've learned.

2 Contrast

About Gloves and Baseballs

Underlying this entire section of the book is a philosophy that we take for granted but that may need to be explained: The shape of an idea matters.

Every idea, or meme, as it spreads, has a sender and receiver. A long time ago, that was a storyteller and an audience; more recently, a writer and a reader or an actor and a television viewer. We used to understand intuitively that, in order for a story to have impact or for an idea to take root in the audience's brains, there had to be resonance. They would have to "get it," of course, but that was easy because the speaker would be able to see the audience directly—there were no books, no tablets, but only the speaker and the listener, and the speaker could easily figure out whether his audience was getting what he was saying. But now we send ideas out blind.

This disconnection between sender and receiver has left us unprepared to truly deliver an effective message unless we've already tried and failed to do so multiple times. This is why the best comedians, for example, are usually the most experienced ones. They've performed many times, and they know when people laugh. They also hear their audience coughing, or heckling, when they fail. They know how to respond in all of these situations to improve how they're perceived.

Yet our interactions with people are increasingly through media. We are leaving tracks for people to check out later on, not screaming in the middle of a town square for an audience to hear right that instant. So we end up presenting our ideas, yes, but we don't think as hard about how they are received, because we don't actually *see* them being received. We don't experience it because we're not there.

The best idea spreaders think hard about how they design and shape their ideas. Consider a baseball game, where the ball is round and the mitt is designed to catch it. Now change the shape of the ball but not the mitt—what happens? Both the throw and the catch become less effective. The idea is caught less often than before. Only the smartest people catch badly designed ideas—and even then, only if they have the patience to do so.

This is the situation we are in now. Almost all successful movies in the modern age work from a template because they know that's what the audience reacts to best. The ones that don't work from this template (screenwriters like Charlie Kaufman come to mind) work through emotional resonance instead. Fiction also follows certain trends—wizards, then vampires, then science fiction, all in a cycle. Business books try to find contrived acronyms to help people remember their ideas. (We are no exception!) There are even world-famous seminars such as Robert McKee's STORY that help people design around these structures because they are so effective.

At the same time, because media creators are increasingly amateurs, we are finding ourselves making the same mistakes beginning writers, filmmakers, storytellers, and businesspeople make because we don't have the right mentors or teachers to prevent us from reinventing the wheel. The audience reads the same blog posts over and over again, while authors are convinced that they have come up with a new idea, even if it's as old as time and not very effective. The environment is reminiscent of the philosophical musings of some teenagers, which we remember having ourselves: "Whoa, what if the green that I see is really your red? Have you ever thought about that? Wild!" Yes, wild indeed. Wildly boring.

But originality is not the point of this exercise. We want our ideas to be connected with, to be caught and thrown again in turn. We need them to be visible against the backdrop of the stadium crowd, so they must have the right color. Finally, their material and weight must be right or they'll get nowhere.

As the environment for our ideas gets more competitive and cluttered, these are no longer trivial subjects. Our friend Alistair Croll once told us that an environment with excess information devours the one thing that information truly demands: attention. Attention is becoming scarce, so we have to use it wisely when we get it.

Here we will learn how to do that. Your idea and its shape are where a lot of your work must go before you release the idea into the world. This work can't be skimped on, and trust us, doing it will lead to the best possible outcome.

An Ecosystem of Ideas

Ideas have never won or lost. Just like any species, they are always competing either until they have achieved a monopoly, like human beings, or until they die out entirely, like the dodo.

It's possible you've never thought of ideas as a competition at all, but as creators we have no choice but to think this way. We have many ideas all the time, and you probably do too. Which to follow, which to wait on, and which to take off life support? Knowing these things is a big part of having your ideas take off.

Consider the three major monotheistic religions: Judaism, Christianity, and Islam. Some may consider them complementary, and it's possible that they are, but in other ways they are actually competing ideas inside the ecosystem of the human brain. They are attempting to pass on to as many people as possible. Only when they have passed to everyone can they be said to have won. Until then, they remain in competition. They want the same turf.

Can an idea really spread like a virus? Some evolutionary biologists, such as Richard Dawkins, think they do exactly that. In his 1976 book *The Selfish Gene*, Dawkins explained how an idea attempts to replicate, just like a life-form, and gave these ideas the name they are known by now: meme (which rhymes with "gene").

A meme is defined by *Merriam-Webster's Dictionary* as "an idea, behavior, or style that spreads from person to person within a culture." The religious examples fall into that category. They are wildly successful ideas that have spread over hundreds of generations. One could even say that they're the most successful ideas of all time.

But successful ideas don't come just from the Fertile Crescent; they come from everywhere and are created every day. They have designs, like any other thing, that help them replicate effectively and take hold in the mind. Like we said earlier, ideas have "shapes," and well-shaped ideas, like tennis balls, can be caught, thrown, and bounced effectively, while ideas with improper shapes don't go far at all.

There's a famous story about Malcolm Gladwell, author of some of the most famous business books of our time, *The Tipping Point*, *Blink*, and *Outliers*. He tells the story of how he would invent words and seed them in his articles—"tipping point" being the most famous example—and then see if other journalists would use these words in their own articles later. He wanted to see if these words would spread on their own. Clearly, some of his ideas did just that. His biggest ideas—the concepts of "10,000 hours," "tipping point," and others—have become concepts so strongly entrenched in Western business culture that lots of people don't even know where they came from. But it's Gladwell who popularized them, and now it is possible for you to do the same.

Just as this is the era of media democracy, it is also the era of idea-creation democracy. In fact, the two naturally come together; to broadcast an idea one must necessarily either have created one or caught one from someone else. You could say that the very purpose of the Web, in fact, is to facilitate connections among ideas and enable others to find them on their own; hyperlinks could have been created for this exact reason.

So we are looking at an era in which more ideas are spreading more often than ever before. Many more ideas will die natural deaths, and faster, because they are exposed to the environment more rapidly. Consider a writer, who has to launch one idea a year, rather than a blogger, who launches an idea every single day. Which one knows what his readers like better? Who will improve faster?

The 2008 video game Spore, created by Will Wright, provides yet another view into how ideas either spread or die. In the game, you create a life-form that evolves in its environment, starting as a microscopic organism and developing into a complex life-form, until it moves beyond its own planet and into space. The game allows you to see how any life-form would "fit" into its environment, either effectively or not. It might multiply quickly or slowly. It might die early or handle its environmental obstacles well and live a long time. All of these things are consequences of the connection between the animal and its environment, the same way an idea's Reach is a consequence of its fit within the ecosystem of its time.

If we begin to consider ideas this way, we can see that each idea does not, by virtue of its being created, deserve a continued existence. Most of our ideas are actually quite bad. Although an idea may fascinate us, it may bore others—go to most dinner parties and you'll realize this quickly enough. So the best "ideators" aren't just creative; in fact, creativity is but a single aspect of idea creation. The rest is a matter of fitting the idea into its environment in an effective way—finding ways for it to spread naturally and quickly and to live beyond its initial contact with its host.

Learning this skill takes a lot of time, a lot of practice, and a lot of screwing up. But it is vital if you intend to transmit anything to the public, to write a book or publish a blog post—even if you want to transmit a piece of wisdom to your children. Know how to do it, and your ideas will naturally fit into the place they are supposed to. Throw out your ideas haphazardly, and they will die quickly in the mind of the recipient.

This means we need a process. We need a methodology. We need a laboratory. Thankfully, the Web has evolved to give you exactly that.

How to Recognize Bad Ideas

The front page of Reddit may be America's new secret pastime.

Since its inception at Y Combinator, a start-up-funding firm, Reddit has been slowly gaining steam, bypassing more famous Web sites such as Web 2.0 once-darling Digg.com. Now its growth is astronomical. Recently, there were over one hundred thousand people on the site at one time. The site has so many users that some of the ideas it transmits have become important cultural artifacts in and of themselves.

Reddit is a social aggregation and news site, which is a fancy way of saying that it's like a newspaper where you can choose how important the stories are. So if you're a Republican, you can see news that interests you higher on the site; likewise if you're a

Democrat or independent. You choose what you see because you, and millions of users like you, control which way the stories go.

Reddit is a site that caters to the Internet community at large. It's not especially representative of the offline world, nor is it always easy to perceive whether you feel welcome. It is, at once, a quirky source of oddities as well as an ad hoc force for social good.

Much of the content that Reddit displays is also "user-generated content," which means that, as on YouTube, most of the stuff on it is created by people on the site. But unlike YouTube, which uses a recommendation engine powered by Amazon.com, Reddit lets you easily find the very bottom of the pile, the worst submissions possible at any time, with one simple click: the "new" button, which gives you access to all new submissions at once.

Visiting Reddit's new-submissions page can be like exposure to an unfiltered, stream-of-consciousness babble from an insane asylum, or like hanging out with your most boring friends all at once. Jokes are falling flat everywhere, and people are saying things that don't make sense, sometimes in languages you don't fully understand. It's filled with the world's self-declared best ideas—only, before they have been judged by everyone else.

Most people don't realize it, but if you read newspapers and visit most mainstream Web sites for your daily influx of news, the only ideas you are exposed to are good ideas—the ideas that have already won. They have been chosen by editors as the best news of the day, and the ideas that were cut have lost. In the gladiatorial ring of ideas, the worst ideas got the thumbs-down. They are dead. And the best ideas are the ones that made the front page, followed by those on page A2, and so on, until you get to the back of the newspaper, where people have paid to include their bad ideas in the form of advertising.

Since most people don't watch an idea's life cycle, they don't know when their idea dies, or why, or how.

But this is changing. Most of the population's first exposure to a laboratory for ideas is now their Facebook time line. For the first time, they can type in any thought they dare say aloud and see how many likes and comments it receives. While limited, this ability has shown people, for the first time, what others think is worthy of sharing and what is not. They are exposed to their own success, or lack thereof, quickly and painlessly, allowing much more feedback than it's possible to receive in normal life.

If your Facebook update is the only content you create online, then your exposure to idea generation and failure is limited. Those who create more stuff—bloggers, Web designers, YouTubers, etc.—naturally understand the process better. The more content they create, they more feedback they are able to receive.

This, incidentally, is why starting out on the Web is so difficult. When there is little feedback, whether it's traffic, comments, Facebook likes, or otherwise, there is no way to know what is working.

The easiest way to bypass this is to obtain an instant audience, such as Reddit's "new" page. It's difficult to handle your idea being voted down into obscurity within minutes, but it can also be enlightening. After all, better to know now whether any merit rests in the stuff we consider funny, interesting, or insightful or whether we should be starting over.

More often than not, when we are exposed to what the world thinks of our ideas, we end up disappointed. But this is a blessing in disguise, because feedback helps produce better ideas faster and more often.

If you are now the owner of a channel, as we have previously expressed, one idea will never be enough. One successful piece of work will never be able to compete, especially as time passes and new ideas enter the marketplace. So you're only as good as your last success. You must create ideas, again and again, and allow them to surpass your previous ones, in both Contrast and Articulation, the two attributes by which we judge any idea. This is not easy. But thankfully, the minds of your potential audience are working for you. They will mostly remember your successful ideas and forget the bad ones. They will recall your greatest successes and forget the mediocre things in between. Experimentation shouldn't be feared but embraced.

Everyone likes a success story, even when it really isn't a success story but a barrage of ideas, some successful and some not. The rest is done in the audience's head, constructing a narrative of success even when that isn't how it happened at all.

This is the real reason your boring ideas don't matter. They won't be remembered; only the good ones will, as well as the massive disasters. Throughout this and the next chapter, we'll do our best to navigate past those as well.

Obvious but Somehow Not Obvious Bad Ideas

We're both biased, very biased, against the way larger organizations run ideas through a kind of dulling/smoothing system, a series of checks and balances, instead of allowing some to go out and be bold.

At the time of this writing, the U.S. fast-food restaurant Burger King is in jeopardy. It has fallen behind Wendy's in the hamburger wars, and we dread to think how it would stack up if you considered Taco Bell and Kentucky Fried Chicken. Not good, we imagine.

Among the litany of bad ideas the company has launched that failed:

Offering table service.

Reintroducing "the King" as a big, creepy, plastic-headed man.

Using advertising offensive to women, because, hey, men are the company's typical buyers.

It goes on. But just look at those three ideas. Table service would be great, except that the expectation for fast-food restaurants is that they are fast, and being helped by a server is the opposite of that. The King was introduced when number one star McDonald's had just minimized Ronald McDonald's appearances in its ads and restaurants; Burger King was bucking the trend, but not in an especially helpful-to-the-buyer way. Offending women because stats prove that men buy more often at Burger King? It's very rare that we'll vote in favor of offending and disqualifying a buying segment that represents more than half of the human race.

How do these ideas get introduced to real people? We don't know for sure. We think it's a combination of forces, however. For one thing, people are often asleep at the wheel and nodding "yes" without looking at things. (Have you ever done that?) And we think sometimes people mistake being shocking for a strategic effort, believing that an idea so far afield has to be good thinking.

This last point is really worth pausing and considering. With what we've written about pattern recognition, it seems that what we're *not* well suited for is understanding when an idea is so far afield that it's foreign, unacceptable, offensive, or the like. How do you guard against that? Later, we will talk about the Impact Equation attribute called Echo. If you can't see even the faintest Echo connection in your idea, it's probably not a good one. That might make for a simple rule of thumb.

Pattern Recognition

Humans are little else but powerful pattern-recognition machines.

We can drive to work and later not even remember how we got there. We can go through rote clicking of links on Wikipedia for hours without realizing where the time went. We learn everything we do by recognizing patterns and then by seeing the breaks.

This is natural, and it's happened since the beginning of time. When you are young, you eat only the food you recognize, and everything else seems strange and repellent. As you get older, the same thing may happen, but somewhere along the way, most people's openness to discovery expands, and they learn a lot. This phase of experimentation is how children learn to walk, run, ride a bike, skateboard, and maybe even build a start-up and change the world.

Pattern recognition is at the core of everything we do. It informs our behavior by showing us what works and what doesn't. It helps us see which of our actions are worth repeating and which are not.

So it's only natural that Contrast, or pattern breaking, becomes one of the most important aspects of the Impact Equation.

In marketingspeak, Contrast is sometimes called the USP, or unique sales proposition. Salespeople and marketers use it to differentiate themselves and their offerings from everyone else. In a world massively saturated with copycat products and services, this is increasingly difficult. It's been said that people in punk bands are just as uniform as everyone else in the world, just within their own subculture—that rebellion is their new conformity.

In other words, every Contrast is conformity somewhere else, inside another environment. Punks who work in an office environment look different and weird unless you're in an advertising agency, where everyone is a "creative" and visible difference is a part of the uniform. When everyone has a tattoo, tattoos cease to stand out and we need more. We need to go further.

But in our ideas we are not looking for universal uniqueness. We are looking only for uniqueness inside our own little field. Thankfully, this is much easier. In order to achieve this, we must consider whom we are attempting to connect with: our ideal reader or audience—whoever is the recipient of the message.

Putting together a cohesive impression of our recipients—where they are from, what age they are, what kind of media they pay attention to, etc.—is critical to developing the message we want to deliver. Only by putting together the audience's world can we discover what Contrast means to them, seeing what it is they'll notice or won't. Attempting to spread a message without thinking about the audience's world is like feeling your way around a room in the dark—that is to say, mostly guesswork, lots of wasted energy, and occasionally a little bruise.

On the other hand, consider the method discussed in the classic business book *Blue Ocean Strategy*, where one is told to simultaneously picture what a category considers to be the "default" state of things—for example, how one conceives of a circus—and how one might create a "blue ocean" of no competition in the space, such as creating a circus like Cirque du Soleil by reaching outside the realms of circus, theater, and entertainment in general.

This is the definition of Contrast—strong positioning so you are creating more value, sometimes with a different price, than most competitors in your category. We have placed Contrast as our multiplier in the Impact Equation because its value cannot be underestimated. When Contrast is low, nothing you do has any impact whatsoever. When you begin to differentiate yourself, however, you create an immediate visibility that is not easily trumped.

Differentiation, however, isn't that simple. If your offering is too similar to the remainder of your category, you are of course invisible, leading you to compete increasingly on price, creating low margins and reducing the value of what you do. However, if you are too dissimilar, you become a radical, making you so vastly different from your competitors that you either offend or repel customers.

Let's consider a few strategies for testing Contrast on your blog, in your business, or anywhere else.

Slow Contrast Increases over Time

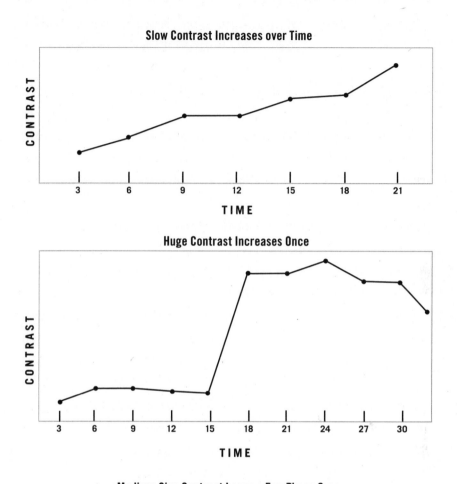

Huge Contrast Increases Once

Medium-Size Contrast Leaps a Few Times Over

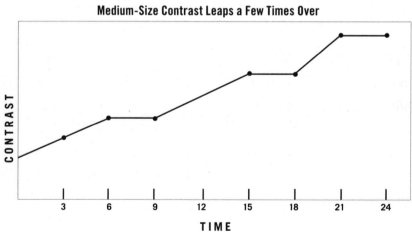

One is to take your time and not risk offending anyone. You're a bookstore that adds coffee or a business blogger who also talks about marketing. No matter what you're offering, this is a small move to make—nothing powerful, but it may make people feel a little better or serve them a little more effectively. However, the changes may end up being so small your clients don't even notice.

Method two is to take a massive leap. Paint your walls pink, add graffiti art, and start blasting death metal in your senior citizens' home. We exaggerate, but our point is that the potential for offense is present and real. Another option could be a drastic reduction in your offering. BeautifulPeople.com might be a great example of this; it's a dating Web site that actively rejects applicants based on "ugliness." We are not kidding.

Third is something in the middle. Medium-size changes, especially considering the status quo of your category, but nothing that might offend. Switching up what you do, perhaps on a regular basis, perhaps arbitrarily.

As you go through the following methods for creating higher Contrast and more ideas, think about how you're going to increase it. Drastically or slowly? While we're at it, we'll give you some ideas to help graph out your audience as well.

Method 1: Have Better Ideas

Why People Have Bad Ideas

One reason many people don't have good ideas is that they were never taught how. The average workplace doesn't have to deal with proper idea-creation methods or produce truly excellent ideas. It never has to see ideas compete against one another, either inside the organization or outside in the ecosystem of ideas. It doesn't truly know how to process good ideas, how to improve them, or how they come to exist. Every part of the equation is missing. "Brainstorming" and its stunted siblings are the only ones present in the room.

It is also never exposed to a marketplace of bad ideas. Just as one never truly knows what is funny until one discovers what is not funny and why (like an experienced comedian), one doesn't truly understand how a successful idea becomes successful until one sees similar ideas fail.

The magic of the amateur, or the beginner, is that he can benefit from beginner's luck—the way random individuals can have massive YouTube successes with tens of millions of views, and so on. (They usually try to re-create their one success over and over again. Sometimes this works, but more often it's just sad.) Everyone else needs a process of constant refinement, of exposure to embarrassment and error, in order to galvanize their mind and keep the learning process going.

After a while, you learn that successful idea creation is not an accident. It follows a process. You must recognize a good idea in your head and then mold it like clay until it's ready for public consumption. As you do this more often, you get better at doing it quickly, until you can become a Seth Godin–esque character, able to send out 150-word snippets that reach one hundred thousand people each day. Becoming this refined isn't obvious, easy, or quick. It takes years. We just want to take you part of the way. Then you can keep refining yourself, all while working on the other Impact Attributes. Do it well enough, and you'll be able to recognize the best ideas and get them out there.

One Framework for Making Better Ideas

Ideas are sometimes tricky and quirky things. They don't just show up when you want them. One way to bring about an idea is to build a simple framework for helping your ideas serve your needs. Let's walk through this.

1. **What's the *goal* of the idea?** First, it's important to understand why you need a new idea in the first place. What are you trying to accomplish? Here's a typical goal: I need to make more money. But herein is the first lesson for having *better* ideas: Be more specific, or it becomes pointless. Maybe you don't just need to make more money; you need to make more money with fewer hours and preferably without as much custom or repeat work.

2. **How does this idea fit my existing framework?** Does it? Let's say your goal is to make more money without as much custom or repeat work, but you're a music tutor. Well, your core job isn't really built for mass production, but if you created a series of online video courses instead, you could accomplish this goal. You can see how it fits together. This is where ideas start to get better.

3. **How much work does this idea add to my life?** One way to have better ideas is to understand how they fit into the framework of your existing life. For instance, Chris had a business idea he thought would be great, but when he did the math, it turned out to be twenty hours of work a week for only a little more revenue. In considering your ideas, you must factor in their impact on the rest of your world.

4. **What will it take to accomplish this idea?** People sometimes have great ideas that start with "Step 1: Buy an NBA basketball team." While this is ambitious, it might be a bit difficult to get past that first step. List what it will take to get your idea going. If possible, list milestones *and* daily bite-

size ways to accomplish it. When we wrote this book, we made the goal one thousand good words a day. With two authors, that gets the book finished in a reasonable amount of time, and it gave us something simple to measure against.

5. What additional resources do I need to make this idea work? This is another area in which you must work out the details. For instance, let's say you are hoping to become a successful real estate professional in Palm Springs, but you've lived your entire life in Mumbai. You should make some connections in Palm Springs so you can start networking and learning about the people and culture. What other resources would you need? You'd need a real estate license for California. You'd need to start finding buyers and sellers. You'd need some contacts. Looking into the resources helps any idea get better.

6. How will I know whether to keep going or quit? One book that we both agree is a critical read for anyone in the business world is *The Lean Startup* by Eric Ries. In this book, he introduces us to the term "pivot," which refers to the moment when a start-up has to decide whether to press on with its original plan or "pivot" and take on a new angle. The same can be done with your own personal ideas, your business ideas, or whatever. How will you know whether to keep following the plan you've created versus pivoting into a new approach?

7. When will I be done? Is the idea temporary? What makes it a "success" or a "failure"? And is there a specific timetable for the idea's usefulness? For instance, if you're thinking about whom you could take to the prom but you're forty, you might have missed your window on that one (we're just saying).

Obviously, this framework doesn't work for every idea, but give it a shot before you throw it out. Let's review the seven questions without our commentary:

1. What's the *goal* of the idea?

2. How does this idea fit my existing framework?

3. How much work does this idea add to my life?

4. What will it take to accomplish this idea?

5. What additional resources do I need to make this idea work?

6. How will I know whether to keep going or quit?

7. When will I be done?

What do you think about this? Does it work for you? Push this up against some of your current ideas and let us know.

Recognizing a Good Idea

Once you've exposed yourself to the bad-idea marketplace by creating many more ideas than usual through mind maps, freewriting, and other methods, you'll have a much better understanding of why certain ideas fail and others do well. Consistently exposing your ideas will refine that skill, but once you've gotten there, how will you know whether you've connected with something that's amazing or something that's simply not bad? This is what we want to help you find out.

Good ideas have many formats, and there have been many books written about how they work, including the amazing *Made to Stick*. But instead of reading assignments, we'll give you a short primer on how ideas are sticky, spreadable, and interesting—in other words, when ideas are really good.

■ Good ideas make you feel . . . something, anything! If an idea leaves you feeling flat, then it is flatlining. You can love it or hate it, but it must make you feel something in order to make you finish reading or watching it, and more so to share it. Julien's book *The Flinch* was short enough to read in an hour, by design, creating a positive feeling in readers along the way and asking them to spread its ideas at the end. It worked, to the tune of thirty-five thousand readers in the first week.

■ Good ideas attach themselves to other concepts in the brain. With existing ideas to grip on to, your idea can hold on to the audience in a much more permanent way. This is what happens when we use CREATE as an acronym for our Impact Attributes—it may seem contrived, but it is simply good idea design. Chris often calls this "giving your idea handles," because it lets people take the concept and make it their own—putting it in their own mind map alongside the concepts that best suit them.

■ Good ideas fulfill a need. Highly efficient ideas help people fill a blank space in their head, whether they know it exists or not. Your opinions may be helpful and interesting, but unless they are specifically useful to your audience, you are not building something of significant or lasting value.

Method 2: Have More Ideas

Idea Storms

First, let us explain that the term "IdeaStorm" is owned by Dell and is loosely based on what LEGO has done with "Mindstorms." The idea is simple: Let everyone share ideas, let everyone vote on ideas, and see what rises to the top. It's brilliant in its simplicity. Just reread this paragraph before going on, and you'll see the value. Many thoughts working on the ideas. Many people able to vote.

This is James Surowiecki's *The Wisdom of Crowds* in action. It's something we understand very well: If there are more ideas, there's a chance we will get to a better answer first. It's a good and proven concept, but there's one caution.

It works much better once the initial or baseline ideas are put in place. In IdeaStorm, Dell invites customers to improve on existing designs or to help fill holes in a system that is already laid out. In Mindstorms, LEGO aficionados communicate augmentations and adjustments to ideas already released.

We have seen no cases where traditional "brainstorming" or its variants work at the *beginning* of the process. Without some sense of context, a framework, or a notion of where to begin, letting loose a lot of ideas into unplotted space isn't effective.

To this point, save the "storms" for when you've got a bit of a framework going, and then let them loose.

Storming Your Ideas

The concept is this: Expose your developed or somewhat developed idea to others to improve it. What's required to make this happen?

- A preexisting idea that feels developed enough to share.

- An idea that can serve others. An idea that serves only you is less likely to be worked upon by anyone other than you.

- An "ecosystem" that allows your idea to be part of something larger, where others can own a part of the experience.

- Flexibility in how other people's ideas can augment yours. It might be an idea that serves a secondary part of your plans, but that might still be quite helpful.

- In most cases, status rewards rather than financial rewards. In the "storm" communities that build around ideas, people more often seek recognition for their ability to solve a problem or create a valuable idea.

There are lots of ways that a system like this can go wrong:

- Trying to build a false or incongruous reward system.

- Seeking help when your idea doesn't have a community.

- Changing the reward system midstream.

- Gumming it all up with improper legal interaction.

- Communicating poorly.

Your Mileage May Vary

If you're fortunate enough to have a community around your product or service or idea, then you can try to start your own kind of idea storm. If not, don't fret. There are still ways to make your ideas better. You'll just have to do more of it yourself.

The Shotgun Blast

There is a lot of garbage on the Internet, true, but it is also becoming the largest repository of amazing information in the world. The garbage that comes out of this process is a by-product, a necessary part of the process that creates genius.

If you personally want to create something amazing, the best strategy is to act like the Internet does. You have to be comfortable with creating garbage in order to have some measure of awesome stuff.

The Web's tolerance for garbage is as high as can be—so anything can go on it—and the best stuff ends up there as a result. Reddit works, as we discussed earlier, because the bad stuff disappears very quickly. Your ability to be comfortable with less-than-perfect content will be directly proportionate to the amazing things you create. In other words, creating today's garbage is an important aspect of creating tomorrow's gold.

This is really about letting the audience decide what is good or bad and curating less. It is a shotgun approach, or as publishers are fond of saying, "Throw everything at the wall and see what sticks." Some publishers have even started to act like this, and Lord knows some of the greatest companies of our time have too.

As you begin this process, prepare to be surprised. The reactions you will get won't be what you expect.

You'll find that the most emotional, most opinionated, and least censored posts become the most liked—though they also tend to be the least well designed.

Once you see what emotion you are able to create and what emotion your audience tends to respond to, it's time to create smart content around those feelings and wrap smart ideas around them.

CONTRAST: A QUICK DEFINITION

When we talk about Contrast in this section, we do it from several angles. In each case, we're talking about how one makes something stand out from everything else. Certain schools require you to wear a uniform every day. If you chose to look different from others, how would you do this while still adhering to the school rules?

You might dye your hair, if that were permissible in the rules. You might tie your tie in a jaunty or perky way. You might choose to accessorize with a very interesting backpack or book cover. Who knows? But that's what we mean by "Contrast."

How Two Different Hotels Use Twitter

We like Christopher Lynn and the team at the Colonnade Hotel in Boston. They are community-minded types and have done a lot to contribute to the Boston-area social media scene. In thinking of a pair of businesses to contrast, we looked up another hotel (chosen absolutely at random) and looked at each of the two hotels' last twenty tweets. Because we are about to criticize the other hotel, we shall remove its name from the comparisons.

Hotel A (not the Colonnade) used its last twenty tweets this way:

■ Inviting people to prebook for an upcoming event.

■ Praising its restaurant's views and food (in that order).

■ Offering a package add-on to get chocolates and other things.

■ Sharing a TwitPic from the hotel.

- Cross-promoting its Facebook page.

- Promoting its wedding offerings.

- Promoting its events for all of 2012.

- Promoting its Google+ page.

- Promoting its cake. (We're not making this up.)

- Sharing a TwitPic from the hotel.

Forget it. We couldn't bear to make you see the next ten tweets. Let's stop at nine.

By contrast, here's what the @Colonnade stream did for its last nine tweets:

- Pointing to a song by the Killers (showing its musical tastes).

- Responding to a guest who tweeted thanks.

- Tweeting more song lyrics.

- Tweeting about the Boston Red Sox (showing community).

- Tweeting twice from the Red Sox game.

- Retweeting a guest praising a recent event there.

- Tweeting again about the Red Sox (again, community related).

- Recommending a JetBlue promotion for Boston-area folks.

- Wishing Fenway Park a happy hundredth birthday.

The first hotel talked all about itself. The Colonnade showed its personality with its musical choices, promoted the Boston Red

Sox celebrating Fenway Park's hundredth year (which was big news for its area), and had a few tweets back and forth with guests. It took us forty-one tweets to find something self-promotional. We thought we saw something about twenty-four tweets in, but it turned out the Colonnade was promoting an independent wedding photographer who was shooting a wedding at the hotel. It promoted her site and praised her for her abilities, thus nudging people to use her for their own projects.

Ask yourself: Which hotel would you rather visit? Now, let's be real. Most people don't think to check the Facebook or Twitter stream of a hotel they're visiting. They might not even care. But by simply looking at the Colonnade's sharp Contrast in *not* promoting itself tirelessly, you get a sense of what you could do with your own business, your own ideas, and your own information sharing or messages.

You can think of Contrast in lots of ways. Look at what competitors say, along with others in your space. Avoid almost all of the words they use. You might use a few specific phrases so search engines find you more easily, but beyond that, don't do it. If your competitors all say, "We value our customer," don't ever say that. If they say, "We are next-generation technology," strike it from your vocabulary.

Think about what else you want to be known for, apart from your primary function. If you're a financial planner, instead of just talking about that, you can say, "I do financial planning for the kinds of people who ride fast motorcycles and think vacations should involve bruises and scars." Can you imagine the difference in which prospects will buy from you?

One interesting way to look at Contrast is that it helps you pre-disqualify potential interactions. Imagine you run a restaurant that serves only premium beer, wine, and spirits. There's not a single drop of common, domestic beer to be found on the premises. If you talked about that online, on your menus, and in other materials, people who preferred premium adult beverages would most certainly identify themselves and those who loved a great can of Pabst Blue Ribbon would know that this wasn't their restaurant.

Eliminate useless or silly words and phrases when considering your Contrast. If you run an accounting firm and you try to tell people that you're accurate and efficient, you're saying what everyone else says. If you say, "We're so good, we do your taxes in *pen*," people will get it and maybe appreciate the humor.

Realize that in life and business, it's always what stands out that gets remembered. If everyone competes on price, but you are the only one raging about your incredible customer service, then that's what we'll remember. (Rackspace Web hosting does this quite well.)

Contrast is understanding more about ideas, understanding their shape, understanding what you need to do to get an idea absorbed by those who need it. We've dedicated a lot of pages to this, because in our minds, if the idea doesn't stand out in a sea of other ideas and thoughts, then it doesn't matter if you've got a great platform and a strong community. This is what needs to happen first.

Ideas and Bravery

Sofia Walker was three years old when she came face-to-face with a large male lion. She had her hands out in front of her and a big smile on her face when the lion reared up and started swiping his paws at her in rapid succession. Yes, there was glass between Sophia and the lion. She was at a zoo in New Zealand. But when you look at the video, you see a three-year-old girl barely flinching when a lion goes into attack mode.

"Bravery" is one of those highly charged words. The moment

someone calls them brave, most people's response is, "Oh no, I'm a coward. I was just brave that one time." We've heard it many times. It's easy for you to say too.

We are all brave sometimes, and we are all cowards other times. The opposite of bravery isn't fear. Fear is built into all that we do. Fear is quite often a helpful tool, so don't ever mistake bravery and fear as opposites. Bravery is simply a noun, a choice.

But what about the bravery of ideas? Contrast is just that. Here's a story to illustrate this.

Chris once worked for a wireless telecommunications company. He was senior project manager on a large computer-systems purchase project that was vital to the company's operations. The company decided to hire a consultant to help run the project, and that consultant was a papered and certified project manager who did things in a different style from Chris. He wrote out vast project plans with minutiae documented at every turn. And the project started slipping.

Soon thereafter, a reasonably new hire (but at the VP level) named Dan Carney came into the picture. Carney took Chris aside one day and asked, "Is this huge, monstrous project plan helpful to you?" Chris shook his head. The consultant was let go. Dan broke the project down a completely different way with Chris.

"Let's keep this to no more than ten lines. Let's have ten-minute status meetings every day on this. The rest of the details belong to those people who own the tasks. Do you actually know better than the Oracle DBAs what they'll have to do to get the database updated?" Chris shook his head. "Great, then just write down their 'supertask' and hold them accountable to it."

There's much more to this story, but the whole project got back on time, every team did exactly what it was supposed to do, no one was ever late to the ten-minute status meetings, and Chris learned an even better way to manage projects than his previous methods, which had been somewhere in between the way of the overdetailed consultant and the minimalist work of Dan Carney.

The whole idea of this method was brave. Carney trusted that the teams involved with the project would own their responsibilities. Carney trusted that a single line item could sum up several hundred detailed tasks. Carney believed that with that little bit of coaching, Chris could complete this crucial project successfully.

The bravery was in bringing a new idea into play that ran counter to the obvious and the acceptable. The bravery came in creating ideas that so strongly contrasted with what had come before that people could have easily dismissed Carney's methods as too simplistic. (In fact, many times in life, the criticism "too simplistic" is applied to a moment of success.)

To work with Contrast is to explore your own bravery.

Bravery Is a Progressive Experience

There's "brave" and there's "psychotic break." When you are exploring your own personal bravery, it's great to feel empowered to stand out and have contrasting ideas and perspectives, but realize that if you spring such ideas dramatically and drastically upon others, they will rarely be perceived well, nor will they be immediately or easily supported.

And yet you can certainly choose to be as brave as you wish.

Eddie Izzard is a brilliant comic from the UK whose style onstage is a frenetic mix of references to Shakespeare, mentions of current events, and strange non sequiturs and segues. Another little detail that sometimes happens with Eddie: He cross-dresses.

"Women wear what they want and so do I," is what Eddie says about it. It's not some kind of act or theatrical issue. He isn't stating a sexual preference with it. He simply prefers to wear women's clothing sometimes.

What was that like the first time? Izzard most certainly wore such clothes in private before he did onstage. So there was a day when he decided (maybe after many days of thinking about it), *Today's the day I'm going to get onstage and wear my dress.* What was that like, you have to wonder? What led up to it? Yet, somehow, Izzard has found a way to make it work.

Now, you might not choose to be a cross-dresser at work, but your creative contrasting idea might be every bit as bold. Maybe there are parts of your personality or your backstory that you've always kept tucked away for fear they would detract from who you are. How might they contribute to what you do?

A Beginner's Guide to Bravery

Here are some thoughts and little tips to practice, to get your ideas to start contrasting and to help you along your way to bravery.

- Your opinion is every bit as valid as anyone else's. (It's amazing how few people believe this.)

- Small victories lead to bigger victories. If you're brave enough to order your food differently off the menu, and nothing bad happens, it prompts you to try bravery elsewhere.

- Accept that you're not always brave. Sometimes you just aren't ready. Don't let that count as a justification. Accept it and move forward.

- Bravery should rarely cost others as much as it costs you, if you fail.

■ Most people's professional struggles can be attributed to breakdowns in their personal bravery. Once you play someone else's game or follow external paths toward a goal, you've surrendered some part of your bravery. Remember to revisit this question if you feel the need.

■ Bravery in your opinions creates Contrast. There's nothing wrong with being a contrarian. That said, pair those contrary thoughts with Echo, to be discussed later. Few people follow a contrarian into battle.

■ Bravery often comes from conflict. Someone says something racist and you call him on it. Someone makes fun of a shirt you like, and you defend it. You might not always stand up. You might not speak out every time, but remember that bravery is won or lost in those moments.

■ Bravery comes from daring to fail.

■ Bravery comes from realizing that mistakes are their own education.

■ Bravery in leadership means accepting that you're not always the smartest one in the room.

■ Bravery in relationships means supporting the other person instead of always pushing your own agenda.

■ Bravery is about giving other ideas air but having your own as well.

There are endless ways we can talk about this, but from Sofia Walker to Dan Carney to Eddie Izzard and now to you, we feel bravery is where it's at. What about you?

Why Smart Content Means Emotional Content

If you are Wikipedia, you can aggregate lots of information and have it be an amazing experience and even a great company. Most people will need another strategy, however.

We strongly believe that the value of a single piece of information is diminishing as more of it becomes available for free, so basing what you do on giving information to others is not as interesting or valuable as presenting it in a human, emotional manner. This is true whether you end up being a smart, highly idiosyncratic rant creator such as Johnny B. Truant or a very personable, compassionate personal-development guru like Jonathan Fields. Using emotion in your content is essential to creating a unique value, and you will need to learn how. This is because information alone rarely sways people. Only feelings do.

Even large brands must create emotional aspects to what they do on the Web. When you watch commercials, the best ones often relate highly personal experiences.

A Super Bowl commercial we saw for Chrysler comes to mind, which featured Eminem and ended with the slogan "Imported from Detroit." By using markers such as the city of Detroit in its ads, Chrysler presents a unique emotional experience that helps people feel the pride Chrysler feels, leading to an empathy no amount of information can buy.

You have to be this way with your best content, or it will happen despite you. If warmth, strength, love, or any other emotion isn't felt through what your channel produces, your audience will be left cold—the exact opposite of what you want. What the famous maxim of the Web "Great content spreads itself" truly means is "Great content makes you want to spread it *yourself*." This can happen by accident, but it most often happens by design.

Emotional Imprint

Contrast is such a powerful force, on the Web and elsewhere, because it is one of the few ways for you to truly leave emotional memories. When trying to convince or sell, you'll notice that most people focus on selling intellectually, using strong arguments they believe will work as effective retorts to their customers' complaints.

The more we worked in marketing, and the more we did presentations and wrote blog posts and launched projects, the more we recognized that information has no impact on people's reactions. Instead of information, people largely react to emotion, and they feel an emotion when they are presented with something different and surprising.

As we began to figure this out, we each began working it out in a different way. Chris started making his work funny, which was a natural extension and brought down people's defenses as they laughed. Julien worked on creating an emotional connection in his work by inspiring people to action. We both noticed this was far more effective than working with bullet points and presenting case studies. At first, we didn't understand why.

Later on, it became obvious to us that one of the reasons this works is that we focus on a different part of an audience's brain, a different wall in their mental fortress, than most people do. Have you ever noticed how the most effective episodes of a television series are those where emotional things happen to the main characters? We are now working with this same theme in mind.

TYING EMOTION TO IDEAS

If you need a car to get you from point A to point B, why spend too much time on that? Find something on Craigslist that runs well enough and is in your price range, and call it good. That's how it works, right? Ideas work best when you can hitch an emotion to them. Look at these two pitches, for example.

Drink Molson because it's a well-made beer.

Get your friends together and celebrate the local watering hole, where you laughed about losing that phone number, where you cried when the Leafs didn't win the cup, and where you first admitted that maybe settling down and having a family wasn't all that bad an idea. Grab a Molson and love your bar the way you love your beer.

Now, which compels you?

You can choose which emotions you want to work with, but also realize that you must be very honest in what you're doing. If you manipulate people, they will never forgive you. The goal, instead, is to build a bridge between the emotion you want them to experience and how your idea best serves that emotion. Make sense?

Extrapolation, Metaphors, and *Ender's Game*

Chris started his business career in customer service for the phone company. Because of this, community and customer satisfaction are at the core of how he preaches business. He lifted the skills he learned in one environment (customer service for telecom customers) and applied them to how a large company might have better business relationships and improved sales. Julien took what he knew and loved about the hip-hop culture and the underground and independent music scene and approached his business pursuits with those mind-sets front and center.

Extrapolation is the ability to squint and blur, to see something and apply it differently, to work without the recipe but use the concepts you've learned. In her book *Find Your Next*, Andrea Kates talks repeatedly about learning not from your competitors but from people in entirely different verticals. What can shoe stores learn from oil-change outlets? That's the goal.

What can the Apple Store teach you about your business? What do Jay-Z's lyrics teach you about improving your communication? How does turning your job as a bag boy in a grocery store into performance art set you up to be a sought-after keynote speaker making great money doing what he learned at age sixteen? Answering questions like these is the goal.

What's a metaphor? Oh, they're for helping people understand things. Metaphors are mental shorthand. (That's pretty much a metaphor, by the way.) They let you explain a concept by stealing from another concept that people can already understand. Here's one of Chris's favorites: "Social media is the telephone. It's no different. A hundred years ago, I'd be telling you, 'You've *got* to get a phone! It's amazing!' And now I'm saying that figuring out Twitter and Google+ is important."

Social media is the telephone. That's a metaphor. You get it. It's fast. It's shorthand.

Learning metaphors helps with Contrast like you wouldn't believe. If you want to build impact, learn and practice to understand metaphors. Learn how to build mental bridges between something that's hard to understand to something that's a lot easier to understand.

In 2009, our concept for a "trust agent" was something like the Walmart greeter for a company. In 2012, our concept is more that it's a concierge. If you know what those two roles mean, you can save yourself 265 pages of reading and you'll have at least the thumbnail of the concept. See? That's what a metaphor can do for you.

TRY IT

Come up with five metaphors for concepts you find yourself struggling to explain. Try to make them as simple as possible and still make sense. The more complex the concept, the better. If you can explain a data center as a giant exploded expensive computer, only bigger, then you're in the right place.

Practice metaphors on friends and acquaintances. The ultimate place would be in situations like on an airplane, when the dreaded "What do you do?" question comes up. Try using a metaphor instead of a job title. You're a project manager? No. "I'm the babysitter at a software company." We promise it'll get you much more interesting responses.

Ender's Game

Okay, if you haven't figured it out yet, we're both nerds. We both use lots of reference points from science fiction, comic books, video games, and other things that will rot your brain. The book *Ender's Game*, by Orson Scott Card, is secretly an instruction manual on how to think about extrapolation and use it to improve Contrast in your own Impact Equation.

The details of the book aren't exactly important to this explanation (aliens threaten the survival of Earth, so a young boy learns how to become a general and possibly save us). What is cool about the book (and if you haven't bookmarked this, written yourself a sticky note, or just Kindle/Nooked the book already, do it now; we'll wait) is that it teaches us to rethink our perspective, to throw away the maps and consider our GPS instead. Perspective, perception, and desired outcome are what you start thinking about while reading *Ender's Game*.

None of this requires that you give a crap about aliens and bugs and laser guns and stuff. Those are the trappings. (This, by the way, is extrapolation. Once you learn how to take the cool nugget from the not-your-thing experience, you're trading in extrapolation.) What's cool is learning that the gate is down, no matter what. (We will not explain what that means, but it's the very kernel of the idea. Read the damned book.)

In your terms, or in business terms, or in Contrast terms, the idea is this: Practice shifting your perspective. Rethink your business as if you had a thousand employees instead of three. What would that change? Someone just did your idea better than you. Now what? You're sick for an entire month. What does that do to your business?

Now blend some extrapolation into the mix. What have you learned in the last few months or years that could apply to your next move? What if you rewrote your résumé to assume you already had your next (very different) role? Rewrite it to explain what you've learned in terms that will relate to the new gig.

Extrapolate and Conquer

This the same as thinking about leverage, except in this case it's mental leverage. Take what you've learned, and move it to the next game. It's building on what you know and helping you find even more Contrast from those around you.

Flip video did this. While other camcorders went with tons and tons and tons of features, Flip made a big fat red button and said, "We are so very easy to use." They iPodded the camcorder space. (Yes, that's now a verb.) Want to extrapolate that same idea again? Head over to the Chipotle restaurant chain and look at its menu. It's one of the simplest chain menus out there. Chipotle might be the Flip video of restaurant experiences.

But bear in mind one vital detail: Choose the wrong idea as the "important" part to extrapolate, and you've got a problem. What matters? What's the real secret of it? That's for you to figure out.

Extrapolation is a power tool. Metaphors are mental shortcuts. The enemy's gate is down.

How McDonald's Added a Hundred Million Dollars to Its Revenue

When you are already the world's largest and most recognized fast-food restaurant, getting sizable growth, the kind that stockholders care about, is no simple feat. But McDonald's took a plan that involved extrapolation, spent heavily to market it, and found one hundred million dollars at the end of the rainbow.

McDonald's was thinking, *Parents come because their kids like the food. What if we gave parents a much more premium coffee experience?* It would never say so out loud, but what it was also thinking was, *We could beat Starbucks up a bit with this, and it's not a normal competitor of ours, so this might have a bigger impact than anyone suspects.* And thus McDonald's launched the McCafé.

This was in store. It was as simple as introducing some new products and as complex as changing the look and feel of the internal colors, building a specific café frontage area inside the restaurants, and cueing people to the mental, social, and emotional concept that McDonald's could indeed present a quality café experience.

Now, earlier we talked about how Burger King failed miserably with its own expansion ideas, and one of these was table service, a bad idea because it adds time. McDonald's knew that having a pure café experience with the kinds of drinks that involve drizzling caramel over frothed cream would add some time to an order. It worked its operational magic to reduce time delay as much as possible. Also, because buyers were quite aware of café time versus fast-food time based on their existing buying habits at a Starbucks, they didn't blink at this context shift.

This is tricky. McDonald's used Contrast to extrapolate its existing product line by building a café experience and selling premium drinks to the tune of a hundred million dollars in the first year of operation. And yet it used Echo (see chapter 7) to help customers realize that this wasn't that different from other café experiences they'd had elsewhere.

CONTRAST: HOW TO IMPROVE

1. Judge the value proposition(s) of the space you are playing in. Consider the blogs you compete against or the products that are above and below you in sales or price. What are they doing for their clients? What offerings define the space?

2. Pan out. Is your value information or emotion? Is it entertainment or education? Pan out to ten thousand feet and ask yourself whether you're really in the lug-nut business. But don't go so high up that you begin to see yourself as a "business solutions" company, unless you're IBM or something. At which point you may not need this book.

3. Where must you compete, and what is critical in this space in order to maintain position? If you lost an entire arm of your products, would you go bankrupt? Whatever offers are critical to your space must stay or, at the very minimum, must be identified.

4. What can be diminished? You panned out; now do the opposite. Focus on each value. What really matters to the audience you are targeting? Do they really care about a given product, or is it a vestigial part of your business? Has your business moved beyond it? What if it were

forced to? What's the worst that could happen? Consider this with each product you offer.

5. What can be eliminated? It's time to make hard decisions. The values you serve up are not equal to all of your customers, and for some they don't even matter. Is a circus without animals still a circus? Cirque du Soleil (and others) think so. In fact, they remove animals and more people want to attend. They can drive ticket prices up by closing in on what really matters to their clients.

Of course, none of this can happen unless you are serious about Contrast. Anyone can differentiate themselves through any offering they have or anything they refuse to offer that their competitors do without thinking.

In other words, what you are creating and what you are competing on is really up to you. You decide what business you're in, how you're going to make a living, and where your profits will come from. It's a strange thought, but it's true. You decide, and you can change anytime you want.

IMPACT EXAMPLE: SKYLANDERS FROM ACTIVISION

A video game where each player can assume the role of one of several mythical characters, each with different powers and abilities, isn't really all that new. Collectible toy figures aren't a new experience. Collectible toy figures that have some kind of online component aren't all that new either.

Blending them together is evidently magical.

Skylanders, from Activision, is at once a multiplayer video-game experience and a real-world toy-collecting game. The toys become your character in the game. Each toy represents a certain character but contains all kinds of onboard information that makes the player's instance of that toy unique. Thus, if Julien takes his Chop Chop character from his house to Chris's house to play a game, Julien's Chop Chop will have different levels and attributes and special powers than Chris's, due to choices made in the game.

Kids and adults alike are calling stores, waiting in long lines, and generally going nuts looking for unique and rare toys for the game system. Retailer Toys "R" Us says that it hasn't seen this kind of passion for a collectible since the 1990s craze around Tamagotchi characters (those little pets in virtual eggs, if you don't recall).

But does Skylanders have the traits required to prove the Impact Equation?

Contrast: Skylanders stands out because the online component of the game is very robust and the toys are very special. In most cases, one of those two items is just the backdrop for the main attraction. This lets the game stand out, as does the fact that your character's experiences are stored in the actual toy, so you can port your play skills and tools to another person's game platform, which is a new paradigm.

Reach: Because this is a video game plus a physical toy, it's difficult to get distribution, and yet it most definitely has a lot of play. Target, Walmart, Toys "R" Us, and many other retailers carry the toys, so they're certainly seeing a lot of attention. Though there's no media property yet, we can envision a cartoon based on the characters cropping up quickly.

Exposure: Frito-Lay signed a deal to feature Skylanders characters on specially marked versions of its products. This kind of Exposure will most certainly push the product out beyond the boundaries of its existing audience and will earn it more attention. Obviously, it benefits Frito-Lay to have this association as well, and the branding match of a snack with a video-game system seems made in heaven.

Articulation: Skylanders is a collaborative fantasy video-game world where your characters are also physical real-world toys that stand as representations of the figures. It's a fairly simple story, and it's not that hard to explain to someone else.

Trust: There's not much with regard to Trust here. Perhaps if Skylanders finds itself in some kind of "hoarding the characters" scandal, or if it makes future versions less compatible with the existing system, there might be some issues, but at the time of this writing, it is at least Trust neutral.

Echo: Players of the game identify with their characters because of the effort they put into improving their skills, tools, and abilities. Chris's daughter, Violette, prefers to use her "Stealth Elf" character above all others, even if another character might be the better fit for a certain challenge. This feels like a powerful Echo.

Skylanders is interesting because the video-game world is a very high-money industry, and creating something truly unique is rare. With Skylanders, it feels like Activision chose to go after a non-video-gamer core market and instead went after collectors and the kinds of people who like Pokémon and Yu-Gi-Oh! cards. Early signs indicate that this is a very successful experience, and we suspect Skylanders has a few more iterative tricks to keep it alive for three more years at the very least.

 3 Articulation

Years ago, Chris was sitting in a very uncomfortable kid's desk chair at a satellite location of a small New England college. A man with meticulously combed hair and a nice suit walked in, put his briefcase down, put his feet up on the desk, laced his hands behind his head, and went into a speech, the details of which Chris can remember almost entirely, verbatim, over a decade later.

Kenneth Hadge taught more solid and actionable ideas about business than Chris had ever learned before. Honestly, the only person who rivals Hadge in the usefulness of his ideas is Sir Richard Branson with his masterful book *Business Stripped Bare*. This instructor, underpaid and representing a very small college with a roomful of not-so-obvious future business leaders, had many great ideas. All of them were simple to remember, useful, and actionable. Here is why Chris remembers this so many years later. Here's a Ken Hadge lesson.

"When someone comes into my office and starts telling me about paradigm-shifting, world-class whatever, I hold up one hand, wait for them to stop talking, and I say, 'Tell it to me like I'm six years old.'"

This is the Ken Hadge method, forever named in this book in tribute. "Tell it to me like I'm six years old."

In the quest for impact, one area that baffles people is thinking that big words equal being understood. Quite often, the opposite is true. If someone trips over your incredible vocabulary, they are not thinking about the idea you've put forth. Instead, they're worried that they don't know the word you used, and they're worried you'll think they're stupid for not knowing it. Even if you yourself had to double-check the word in the dictionary before using it, it's going to sit there like an obvious adornment on an otherwise simple effort.

Use small words. Use many if you have to (though fewer is better). This is the method. This is how people connect with your ideas and learn to make them their own. To have impact, a simple phrase, especially one that contrasts against people's expectations, is better.

Nike said, "Just do it." It didn't say, "Execute and energize your peak performance." Can you imagine that as their slogan? And yet many a corporation uses such words.

Does Simplicity Play to the Lowest Common Denominator?

If I talk to the stupidest person in the room, am I risking the rest of the audience? Using small words doesn't attract small minds. Small words are a way to seed ideas in anyone's mind without creating unnecessary barriers.

The truth is this: Your choice of words and your choice of description aren't the secret sauce of the idea. They are the wind that carries the paper airplane to its destination. Your words must serve the idea. That's all.

In researching this part of the book, we thought we'd go find a pithy sentence from an actual six-year-old and point out that it's obviously well said. That would really have summed up our point. What we found, instead, was interesting. There are many Web sites and many jokes and many hours spent trying to cast children saying something innocently for the sake of a joke. In each of these cases, the child is portrayed as a simpleton and not the creative mind he or she truly is.

That perception, written repeatedly into jokes, may be an even better illustrator of the fear that "Tell it to me like I'm six years old" will lead people to think simple thoughts. So let's go about this another way.

Exercise: Use Small Words

Take a moment and write answers to the following exercises, using no more than twenty words of no more than two syllables. Try it. Seriously. Don't just skip the section and keep reading. Anyone could do that.

■ Describe what you do for work. Describe what your company does.

_____

_____

_____

_____

_____

■ Describe the movie *The Matrix*.

_____

_____

_____

_____

_____

■ If we gave you five million dollars, what would you do
with it?

_____

_____

_____

_____

_____

■ What is your personal philosophy?

_____

_____

_____

_____

_____

■ What do you want most in a new hire or colleague?

_____

_____

_____

_____

_____

It's tricky, isn't it? The urge to use large words or complicated
explanations is worth policing. If you can't say something simply,
what are the odds that someone else will understand it any better?

Keep Your Ears and Thoughts Open for Moments of Small Words and Large Ideas

Examples of and coaching on how to better articulate your ideas
are all around you.

While writing this part, Chris went away to a yoga retreat. His
instructor, Rolf Gates (who is also a kind of Ken Hadge), explained

a complex philosophical and psychological term, *asmita,* as the "mind made me." The premise has something to do with how your ego builds all kinds of prisons for you. For instance, your belief that you will never get out of debt is a prison you created for yourself. There's obviously no real reason why this should be true. But think of that simple phrase: "mind made me." I am the "me" that my mind has created, and once I accept this, the premise goes, I should be able to step outside that perspective and learn more.

Now take that concept, built off those three words (all one syllable, by the way), and try explaining that to your kid. Talk about what it means to be self-censoring in language a kid would understand. Practice this.

The more you learn how to express yourself using the Ken Hadge method, the more you'll be able to deliver a strong message. We'll talk about another idea on Articulation that builds on this.

THE FIERCE EDITOR

How many words do you need to express your idea? Here's a hint: That last sentence was probably too long. Part of learning Articulation is learning which words to choose. Another is learning which words to lose. And yet another is understanding when you have to explain something a little bit more for it to make sense and be useful. We need a fierce editor, and barring hiring someone for this, you've got the job.

We need venture no further than our in-box to see examples of all three situations. Look at your sent items. Have you sent a long e-mail that could've been pared down to a hundred or fewer words and gotten your point across? Have you sent an e-mail using too few words that resulted in a ping-pong game requiring you to check your in-box ten times? Now is the time to fix these problems.

One of our favorite Web sites, http://two.sentenc.es/, focuses on this concept by asking senders of all e-mail to restrict themselves to text message–like lengths. When concepts don't fit into this structure, they can be addressed in a phone conversation, a blog post, or some other form of media. But the larger point is that format should be dictated by need, and restrictions can actually help you become better with your message.

Articulation in Action: Chipotle

Have you been to a Chipotle restaurant? The process is spread across four big signs behind the cash register and preparation area: "ORDER" (a particular format for serving the food), "WITH" (a meat type or vegetarian), "SALSAS" (sauces and what they cost), and "EXTRAS" (chips and guacamole). You can figure out rather quickly how to order. There are only five or six ways to do it. There are only four meat options and one vegetarian in "WITH." You can pick a few sauces and extras. It's a flow. The flow exists on the boards. It's somehow even easier than the typical fast-food menu.

But this language and messaging is in everything Chipotle does. Have you seen its advertising? Swing by Chipotle.com and click the "Back to the Start" link (if it's still there when you finally read this book). It tells a video story of Chipotle's commitment to fresh food. It is articulate and simple, told with cute-but-vibrant animation talking about why fresh and local food is better for all parties. It's clear that Chipotle wants its ideas heard, understood, and embraced as our own.

Can you articulate what you sell in just a few simple boards with very few words? If not, why not?

Connecting the Dots

One of the main reasons there is still a huge difference between a blog post and a complete, mainstream book is that a book must work harder, much harder in fact, at connecting the dots.

The very concept of connecting the dots is human. It's something that can't be done by machines but that humans are very good at. Think about it. Where a human being could fill in the blanks and see a lion after putting some of the dots together, a machine might not see anything. So a big part of creating clarity in your idea is connecting the right dots.

A group of blog posts could be a disparate set of ideas that don't necessarily mesh well. Publishing them as a book would be like adding the details of a painting before the big picture, like adding stars before painting in a sky, or painting a tree, a river, and a mountain but nothing in between to make them into a landscape. As short ideas, they each work well, but they're nothing you could sell on the art market or hang in a museum (unless the drawing were part of a larger story). Books, or any final, completed media, have high Articulation because they explicitly connect the dots among multiple ideas in order to create a final, concrete explanation.

Connecting the dots gives you a ten-thousand-foot view. It brings together a whole picture, which is much more easily comprehensible. It lets you start at the beginning instead of in the middle, making it less likely you'll end up confused by what's going on. In other words, it gives your big idea, your marketing campaign—whatever it is you're working on—a sense of context.

Let's take an example. For years, a real estate agent's blog could talk about housing prices, renovations of kitchens and bathrooms, backyards, and different neighborhoods. Only later could this become a cohesive, sellable idea such as "The Complete Guide to

Selling Your House in Boston." This final product could have connections that are lacking in each small tip you would find on the blog or get from the agent in person.

But adding length and depth isn't the only way to connect ideas into a collective, larger whole. If we were to simply collect every fact about the American Civil War into a book, for example, we would have something that could easily fill a thousand or more pages. So one of the most important skills in connecting the dots isn't just putting everything together, which can be done by machines. It's the process of *synthesis*, which requires a smart human or two to look at the whole and decide what really matters, what needs to be kept, what needs to be removed, and what two or more pieces can simply be combined into a new whole. In the book *Five Minds for the Future*, Harvard professor Howard Gardner calls synthesis one of the five critical skills necessary to distinguish yourself from both peers and machines.

Here's a quick guide to connecting the dots to help you create a better final portrait of your idea.

1. **Get data from more varied sources.** It's easy to read everything that everyone in real estate has already read and create a product from it, but that's the product of a machine, not a human being. But if you're making a product like *How Harry Potter Is Like Real Estate*, then you have a bunch of data sources that other people haven't considered. And connecting weird dots isn't just about grabbing a bunch of data from unexpected places. It's also how humor works—the unexpected, when well timed, is usually very funny.

2. **Find unexpected patterns.** There are patterns everywhere. If you look carefully you can see, for example, correlations

between how well the economy is doing and the size of shoulder pads in suit jackets. Putting together different concepts under the umbrella of a pattern is what we did with this book, for example. This relates to number 1 as well, because finding patterns means getting more data from more places.

3. **Remove the irrelevant.** Does your work need to have absolutely every example, or can many be removed if you find one perfect example? The problem with lots of the work out there is that it relates the same thing again and again without adding new information. This is subject to opinion, of course, but in many cases finding patterns (number 2) can allow you to remove many repetitive examples and replace them with a single one.

4. **Add random data.** The human brain is an amazing pattern-recognition machine. If you ever need an idea for anything whatsoever or need to see an old idea in a new light, attempt to add random data and see how your mind connects it to the old stuff. This is a known technique discussed by lots of creatives, such as Edward de Bono, as well as Brian Eno with his Oblique Strategies cards.

There are more methods, but they all focus on the same idea. Take disparate concepts and connect them. Take a look at what the new, combined concept is like. Give it a name and simplify it. Then do it again, somewhere else, until the concept is simple and perfect.

#

If you're like us, you probably started on the Web quite a few years ago. You may blog, but intermittently. You're not "a writer" necessarily, or at least you don't call yourself one. You may have a university degree in literature or something, which means you had to write long essays at some point, but that was a long time ago. You're definitely no longer accustomed to writing on a regular basis, and this probably means you think you're terrible at it—and hey, you may be right!

We're not here to berate you about not writing, but we will tell you this: Writing is now one of the few skills you must have—and we really mean "must" here—for the twenty-first century.

Think about it: More and more of our content is consumed online. It gets sent to your mobile phone, your tablet, or your computer. We consume more written media than we ever have in history. Do you sincerely think this trend is going to suddenly reverse itself? It's time for all of us to become master copywriters. Many Web aficionados are already doing it. They're learning to master written sales techniques that get amazing results for any half-decent product they come across. As they get better at it, in some cases they are literally creating their own jobs by becoming better salespeople and persuaders.

Meanwhile most of us are sitting around, passively *consuming* content instead of *creating* it. Actually, it makes us kind of angry just thinking about the wasted potential. Maybe it has the same effect on you. We hope so, because it really is that important to learn.

Writing proper, excellent copy is going to be one of the most important tools in your attempt to conquer the world with the stuff you make. If you can write well and sell well, you can build an audience and make requests of them more often.

If you don't know how to do these things, though, you'll find yourself more dependent on others. Your channel won't get much attention and you won't know how to develop it. Or even if you have one with a significant audience, you won't know how to sell them something. So you must learn to convince with your words.

To do this, you really have to become a master of language. This takes a lot of practice, and we can't do the work for you. So for now, here are some 101-level tips.

1. Learn to freaking spell. Does this really need an explanation? Sincerely, this is important. Misspellings have a huge impact on credibility (a factor in Trust, discussed later). At the minimum, use a spell-checker. This is basic.

2. Expand your vocabulary. The magic of e-readers is that they typically include a dictionary. Click and highlight and you have a definition, instantly. How better to improve your understanding of your own language? Imagine how clunky it was to do this a hundred years ago and rejoice. Any time you don't know a word, don't think twice. Just do it.

3. Study the masters. Copywriters have sold hundreds of thousands of books to people like you and me because selling through writing is their art form. They have perfected it to such a degree that the writing seems natural and easy, all the while subtly convincing you. So study them!

4. Copy a masterwork. When Julien first remarked on his blog that he was doing this, it seemed nuts (and the comments said so). But some of the best-known writers of our time have done it. Haruki Murakami has translated a ton of English-language works into Japanese and is now considered one of the world's greatest living writers. And Hunter S. Thompson, during his tenure at *Time* magazine, typed out Ernest Hemingway's and F. Scott Fitzgerald's books on a typewriter. Copying a masterwork isn't as crazy as it seems.

5. Write endlessly. Nothing works better to improve writing than making time for it every day. Free yourself from the constraints of perfectionism by writing something you've deliberately decided you'll never read ever again or perhaps even decided to destroy afterward. Or, practice free-form writing and then editing afterward, but not together—they are usually incompatible.

Too Many Ideas

We often hear from people that they have "too many ideas." They might start working on an idea to build a Web site that helps bands find better rehearsal spaces, but before they finish, they get a new idea to import different types of tea from Barbados and begin working on an import/export business. Midway through that, they have a great idea for how to really improve Netflix, if only they could meet the right person and talk about it.

Everyone can suffer from this, if they choose to let their ideas run rampant. Chris did this a lot in late 2010 and into 2011, and it had quite a negative impact on his business. He would run with something, feeling very entrepreneurial about it, and never quite get the execution just right before he started in on something else. Julien's had his share of ideas that have started and stopped too. When exposed to the Web, it's natural. Lots of ideas seem exciting, but the ability to focus is really what matters.

Having too many great ideas is really part of the process. From there, you must pick an idea or a few ideas and work them from raw thought into something that might deliver value. And again, you can look at "idea" as meaning "project" or "thought you want to communicate" or "mission" or many other things. It all works out the same.

Having too many ideas is a starting point. Next you might decide upon a framework to determine which ideas are worth acting upon. That's where most people miss a step.

There are many ways to tackle this, and which is best ultimately depends on what types of ideas you're talking about and what your goals are. Let's look at a few frameworks and talk about how they might work for you.

Business Ideas

If you want a way to evaluate business ideas, you might build a framework like this:

- Does this idea fit our mission and goals for the year and beyond?

- Is the new idea revenue generating (or cost cutting)?

- What would it take (money/time/resources) to get the idea launched?

- Who would champion this idea and do they have time?

- Assuming we're working at 100 percent capacity right now, what would have to *go* to make room for this idea?

- How much money could we potentially make (a conservative estimate), and is it worth it?

Looking at that set of questions, you can see how to phase out "too many ideas." You might have an idea that meets a few of the above criteria, but you'll see rather quickly why it won't be worth pursuing if it doesn't do well on the others. If you do this often enough, you'll end up with just the correct amount of ideas, *and* the right ones.

Creative Ideas

If you're an artist or musician or some other creative role, maybe you need a way to determine whether to pursue a project idea. Your determining factors might be different. Let's look at a sampling.

■ Does this idea connect with any of the themes of my work?

■ Does this idea stretch me as an artist, or is it a repetition?

■ Can I use my skills to execute this idea?

■ How much time and other materials are involved in this idea?

■ Do I care whether this idea is salable or not?

The best possible way to sift through the abundance of ideas in your head is to work through a framework of questions that will help you determine what works best for you and your pursuits. Again, the questions really will vary. A creative person might not care whether a project is revenue generating but might care a great deal about whether an idea stretches his or her skills or abilities.

Do Your Ideas Have Any Longevity?

Another problem with having too many ideas is that we have to be very conscious of the value of time. You might have a great idea, think it through, give it a pass through your framework, and launch it to your platform. But what if you don't give it enough time to get off the ground? Or, in another time-related perspective, what if your idea is only really viable for a brief amount of time?

Thinking through the potential longevity of an idea is another good way to "gate" these opportunities and decide whether or not to give them a go. Chris once launched a project where he intended to shoot video reviews during all his business travels. The project presumed that Chris would be on the road quite often (which at the moment was true). Shortly afterward, Chris reduced his time on the road, and the project collapsed. If he'd thought about the idea's long-term staying power, he might not have launched the project and left another orphaned site out there on the Web.

Thinking through the timing of ideas will help you reduce "too many ideas" to a workable number.

Story, Packaging, and Too Many Ideas

Imagine you're tasked with creating a movie. You decide it should have giant robots. You then decide it should also have Greek gods and mythology. Then you add 1930s-style gangsters. Finally, you determine it should be a musical. Odds are, it won't work.

The same is true of having too many ideas. It's important to apply constraints to what you're doing. Said another way: By sticking to one strong theme or story, you'll have a better chance of limiting your ideas to those that are more promising.

The beauty of constraints is that they let you work within a certain set of parameters and cull extraneous "noise." If you decide to improve your physical health over the next several months by taking up running and body-weight exercises, it might not be useful to also take up basketball. You might decide to rule out the idea of getting a new mountain bike, because that isn't running, nor is it body-weight exercises.

Similarly, with a bigger idea, you can ask whether it fits the story you intend to tell. If you've decided to focus your efforts on selling video projects to big companies, starting a small business consultancy doesn't match. This kind of story-based thinking allows you to rule out some of those "too many ideas" quite easily.

#

At the time of this writing, tablet computers and smart phones have overtaken both laptops and desktops as the communication and consumption devices of choice. People are no longer comfortably reading your very long and rambling e-mail at their desk. They are reading it on the way to the bathroom in between meetings. They are reading it while on hold for a conference call. They are almost always reading it in a distracted and time-crunched moment of the day.

Think about yourself: That's when *you* read e-mails now, right? You almost never sit down with a steaming mug of coffee, give a delighted sigh of contentment, stretch your neck muscles, and dig into your in-box. Instead, you quickly scan to make sure the boss or your clients or your significant other haven't thrown something new on your plate.

Worse still, if the mail you've sent to someone else was too long, they've clicked it as read without finishing it, and now it's sitting in the gray, no-longer-bold, below-the-interesting-and-unread-stuff no-man's-land part of the in-box (or worse, it's filed away!). You can forget about a response if that's where your mail landed.

But what happened? Why did the recipient forget about you? Don't you deserve at least the courtesy of a response?

Let's ask some questions:

❑ Was your subject line obvious and actionable? Could the recipient answer based almost entirely on it?

❑ Did you put the most important part of the e-mail in the first paragraph?

❑ Did you end the e-mail with the one question that was most important?

❑ Was there one "ask" in that e-mail or more than one?

❑ Was the e-mail HTML formatted and sent via a "donotreply@" e-mail address? (That is, was it a newsletter?)

❑ Had you messaged the recipient recently (within a few months) without making an ask?

❑ Was the e-mail fewer than three hundred words?

❑ Could the recipient read it in under thirty seconds?

There are several reasons why people have stopped responding to e-mail in a timely fashion, and most of them revolve around too much e-mail in their box and e-mail becoming less and less easy to answer. Hint: If SMS text messaging is on the rise, why would you still send 1,400-word e-mails?

Brevity and Articulation

Making a point is easier if you're brief. Sometimes doing this makes people nervous. Teachers told them to write long, flowing sentences that show off their ability to produce great prose that stacks up against the likes of Herman Melville and prove, once and for all, that they understand grammar.

Phooey. Write brief sentences. Need help getting into it? Read *The Shipping News* by Annie Proulx. No, it has nothing to do with business. It's fiction. It's a few years old at this point. Whatever. It will cure you of the need to write superlong sentences.

The rule of grammar and paragraphs is to write three sentences per paragraph at minimum.

Phooey part two.

Welcome to the land of skimmers. If your idea is packed into a dense thicket of words, it's lost. The faster you can shave off the fat and get to the point, the faster you'll see your e-mail response rate go back up.

Articulation and brevity go hand in hand. If someone is to understand your idea, it has to be in a very tight package.

Could you say it in three words?

It's much harder than you think to do this, by the way. For example, Chris's company, Human Business Works, is a strategic advisory company that helps midsize to large businesses with customer acquisition via the digital channel. Blah blah blah. Say that in three words?

"Digital marketing strategy." It's a whole lot harder to sell with just those three words. That said, if we put that in the first line of an e-mail, it's a lot more likely to get read than blabber about customer acquisition and the rest of it. See how this works?

If you can't simplify words, lines, and syntax and make your writing clearer for people to respond to, you are doomed.

Do you see how we wrote this section mostly to demonstrate what we're aiming for in your e-mail efforts? (If you're listening to the audio program, that's probably a "no," but pretend we've written very brief, simple, punchy sentences with lots of tiny paragraphs instead of longer ones. Fair?)

Articulation will help you see responses.

CLARITY AS A FORM OF CONTRAST

If you're good enough at it, it's possible that high Articulation (or clarity) in your message may in fact be enough of a differentiator to put you over the top—from invisible to visible, from zero impact to high impact.

When Stephen Hawking came out with *A Brief History of Time*, there had never before been such a clear expression of how the universe and time work. Yet the ideas were not new. Only their expression and packaging were. In this case, it was enough.

Consider the originally submitted title, *From Big Bang to Black Holes*. It clearly conveys what the book is about yet leaves you with no impression of the subject's grandeur. Graphics inside help you truly understand how the four dimensions work. Opening it leaves you with the immediate impression that, yes, you can learn this stuff.

Combined with his important brand in the space (no pun intended), Hawking was able to create the first mass-market physics book, eventually selling over ten million copies and staying on best-seller lists for four years.

Here's how to use high clarity to differentiate yourself.

Value clarification: "How to Gain a Thousand Twitter Followers in One Hour." Putting the value proposition in the title often tells people exactly what they need to hear. If this is something your audience has been meaning to figure out, they'll see it and care immediately. So you can gain an advantage just by clarifying.

Data visualization: If 2008 was perhaps the year of the top-ten list on the Web, 2011 could have been called the year of the infographic. Known to initiates as data visualization, infographics have caught on in a big way on the Web because of their ability to clarify data (and sometimes mislead with it, actually). Will they still work by the time you have your hands on this? Test them out and see.

Condensed or expanded content: Make what you do extremely concise and clear or extremely long and profoundly explained. Either method is a form of clarity if properly used. Viperchill.com, a blog run by the South African Glen Allsopp, produces material so long that his twenty thousand subscribers can't help but feel that every article is a super-comprehensive, well-researched guide (and it is). On the other end of the spectrum, Seth Godin produces content so dense that practically every line is spreadable on its own without further explanation. Either of these options is better than middle of the road, where nothing much happens that's exceptional at all.

"Hey, I've Got an Idea"

Because we're both in business for ourselves and seem reasonably successful, friends and strangers alike want to tell us their business ideas. Quite often, they're hoping for validation, and then, a lot of times, they ask us to participate in some way. (We usually have to decline, because our plates are full.) In hearing a lot of these ideas, we've come to know a bit about how some people frame their concept of a business.

If I Need It, Someone Else Will Too

We hear ideas like this one all the time: "I was in the market for a bonsai tree, and then I realized that there aren't really any good bonsai tree–selection Web sites out there, ones that really cater to someone interested in starting from scratch. So I'm going to start that business." Okay, before we go too far, it's important to realize that there's a niche for everyone, and before you discount someone's business idea because it seems too quirky, remember that there are many people out there who are completely successful doing strange businesses you wouldn't believe. And yet there are some points to consider.

An idea for a business isn't good just because you yourself have a need. You might have to validate whether or not others are showing signs of the same need. However, to paraphrase Henry Ford, most people thought they needed faster horses, not automobiles. You might not be able to find evidence that people have a need like yours. You might have to create a prototype and get a few people to test the concept. And "a few people" might mean thousands. It depends on the product or service.

There are other ways to get into a bit of a bind when thinking about business ideas.

I Really Understand These People, so I Can Sell to Them

We've lost track of how many people (usually in their twenties) tell us about their ideas to help bands. We used to be a lot more polite while listening to these ideas, but after a while, they all kind of blur. Our most common answer when we're given a chance to reply: "Bands don't have money."

Quite simply, just because you are from the same demographic you're hoping to sell to or believe you're attuned to a certain market segment, that doesn't mean your idea will have business value. Bands, as we've pointed out, don't have money. If you've created the ultimate band-promotion site (which has been done successfully several times, by the way), you'll have to find a way to extract money from some other segment. Think just a moment longer about this example. Audiences don't like to pay. Heck, they barely like to pay for music. Will the record labels pay? Not likely. Not often. They have a "not invented here" bias problem. So what do you have? An amazing idea that won't make you money.

I'm Really Good at This, so I Can Do a Business

We feel like we're stealing from Michael Gerber's E-Myth books, but hey, if you're a great cook, it doesn't mean you're a great businessperson. The skill set required to cook has nothing to do with the skills required to market a restaurant, get more customers in, and improve your margins while not watering down your product.

There are people who are really good at painting portraits or quirky street art, but there's a reason people talk about being a "starving artist." Art either sells remarkably well or it doesn't. And you don't have time to sell posthumously.

There are many variations on this particular idea problem.

People tend to mistake their aptitude as a shoo-in for business success. There really are some great accordion players out there. We can name one: Weird Al. See where we're headed with this one?

Ways to Reshape Your Business Ideas

One easy way to determine whether your business idea is potentially viable is to run through this quick checklist:

❏ Do I have a market for this? Do I know how to reach the people who might want this?

❏ Do I have the resources and time and proclivity to do this? (Remember your goals from part 1, and ask if this aligns with them.)

❏ Is this something people will pay for? (This one often seems to be skipped in people's assessments.)

❏ How sustainable is this business? Can I do it for a while?

❏ Is this business salable? Can I turn it over to someone later on?

You can choose to answer these questions however you like. If you're part of a larger company, you might modify them to meet your needs. If you are a sole proprietor or the owner of a smaller business, you might face these questions quite often. Remember that if you replace "business idea" with "new product or service," a lot of the same questions apply to established companies.

Chris hasn't been very successful at building salable businesses. His business ideas tend to revolve around his abilities and experience, which obviously don't translate to something one can walk away from. Julien has been fortunate in this regard. But it's definitely something to consider, if it's your business and you want to find ways to grow your potential.

Don't Get Discouraged

There are dozens (hundreds? thousands?) of people who will tell you that your idea will never work. There are just as many people who believe you are doing the same thing that others have done before. Every time you hear this, smile politely. There were many airlines when Sir Richard Branson launched Virgin, and he did great. There were many people selling MP3 players when Apple (then failing and most definitely not a "sure thing") launched the iPod. There were many people selling personal-improvement seminars and educational materials when Tony Robbins did so and went on to become wildly successful.

For every person who tells you why you can't accomplish a business idea, including us, be true to yourself. There are so many rejection-letter-to-now-very-obviously-successful-person stories out there that we refuse to list them here. Any one of them tells the same story: Hundreds of people said this person couldn't do it, and then they went on to be one of the most amazing whatevers in the history of that segment.

That can be you. Work on your idea. Work on building your platform. Understand the human element. Build your own Impact Equation around all this, and you'll find a way to make ideas that matter.

#

People who doodle get a bad rap. Are you a doodler? We are. If anyone has ever questioned whether you were paying attention because you were shading your stick-man Batman in the margin, never fear. We think there are many ways to use visual thinking to improve your ideas.

Have you tried mind mapping yet? This is the act of moving your ideas around visually. It's a great way to open up your thought processes to the logical flow of ideas.

The basic technique is that you take a blank piece of paper (there are also hundreds of software applications written for this same function—we use XMind and MindNode), and you draw a smallish oval in the middle of the page. Here you put your primary idea. Maybe it's "popular Web video show."

From that main circle, draw a line or a branch and pop up another oval, where you might put down "barriers to success." From *that* branch, add another oval that lists "lack of funds," "no skill in making video," "really ugly looking," and the like, one idea per oval.

Then go in another direction with a new branch, and write "subjects for video." Splitting up that branch into its many possibilities, begin with writing "football" and split that up into "NFL" and "college." Then go back to your "subject" options and write "hockey" and split that one up into its branches as well.

Mind mapping is basically visual note taking that ends up significantly more powerful than traditional methods. It lets you think through ideas in a visual way, work through possibilities, and see all their contingencies. You can create mind maps with many different uses. You can build them to test out an idea, to make sure you've thought through an idea, to decide what else will need to happen for an idea to be successful, and more.

Julien uses mind maps to map out blog posts and with games he runs with friends. They work because they fit the way the brain has ideas, by connecting one to another. They're also much better than simply thinking because they allow you to go back to concepts you've left behind and develop them later.

As Chris started adding to this part of the book, he realized that his mind-mapping software was open. In it was a little map to think about success:

The thoughts that accompany this mind map were about what it might take to be successful. Are you an actor or a spectator? Are you a lifelong learner or did you "drop out" after you finished your degree? Are you a context shifter or a trench worker (do you see the big picture or details)? Are you a wealth builder (someone who uses money to improve the world) or a bargain hunter (someone worried about scarcity)?

That was one side. On the other side Chris wrote about what the external functions of this person would have to be. He or she would have to believe that his or her secondary function in life was marketing, sales, and customer service to his or her idea. He or she would have to be an expert storyteller who understands how to bring an idea to the campfire (hey, yet another metaphor), and this person would have to be a hero maker, meaning that to truly succeed, one must help others succeed. Finally, a truly successful person must have a strong "no" gate: the ability to say no to opportunities or paths that detract from his or her success.

Using mind maps allows you to build a visual of your ideas. You can do this with paper and a pen. You can do this by drawing. You can think visually in lots of ways. If you want a really interesting book on this process that extends into using visual thinking and games to improve your business, check out *Gamestorming* by Dave Gray, Sunni Brown, and James Macanufo (see also http://www.gogamestorm.com/). Also be sure to get into Chuck Frey's Web site (http://www.innovationtools.com/), as he's the leading authority on all things mind mapping and our go-to person for learning what's new and interesting in that world.

But don't stop there. Visual thinking can take many forms. And opening your head up to new ways of forming ideas is just as important as everything else in this book.

Our buddies Hugh MacLeod (gapingvoid.com) and Mars Dorian (marsdorian.com) can boil fascinating ideas down to the back of business cards. Their styles of visual thinking can certainly give you a new way of looking at your idea. And though we're writing about mind maps specifically, realize that you can get there in many ways. How would a little cartoon change your perspective? Could the "voice" of the cartoon be the voice you're not yet willing to claim as your own?

What if your mind maps were storyboards instead?

Karen J Lloyd (http://karenjlloyd.com/) writes about storyboarding on her blog and points out that it isn't just for artists anymore. You might just be someone with a business question the mind map didn't solve. Why not try "telling the story" with a storyboard?

Not sure how to apply that one? Think about it. What if you were debating whether to move cross-country and take a new job in a town where you have no roots? What would that story look like drawn out in boards? You could talk about what it's like to reestablish a local network of friends. You can talk about what babysitting issues might arise now that you don't live near your parents. See how the drawing process shifts your thoughts into a different angle?

Though we both write books, blogs, and other linear, narrative works, we both branch into a variety of types of visual thinking when we consider how to improve our impact. The written sentence can be freeing, such as when you're journaling to "talk onto paper," but it can also be limiting, as you must use a certain syntax that is already laden with presumptions. Said another way: It's sometimes harder to see the alternatives to an opportunity or a challenge if you're using the written form.

Open your possibilities. Try mind mapping. See what other visual-thinking methods might apply to you. What could it hurt?

Discovering the Core Message

In his amazing book *Understanding Comics*, author and illustrator Scott McCloud explains how emotions get illustrated. He shows how, when your face shows emotion, it usually isn't a simple expression but a combination of two other simpler feelings. For example, surprise is a combination of fear (eyebrows up) and shock (mouth wide open).

Lots of concepts can be dissected this way—divided in two to make them easier to understand. The movie *Alien* was first pitched to studio executives as "*Jaws* in space," for example. Likewise, we could extend this idea outward, coming up with other "*Jaws* in . . ." ideas, such as "*Jaws* in Africa." (This might end up being *The Ghost and the Darkness*, starring Val Kilmer, for example.)

You can use this same method to help you understand yourself, your company, and your project a little better. If you work at it hard enough, you may even get to the core of your message, what you are really about—and expressing it to others will become infinitely easier.

Method 1: The Triangle Method

Imagine a triangle. If you are a company, then each point on the triangle is also a company. If you're an individual, or if you have a blog, then each point becomes an individual or a blog, respectively. In the middle of this triangle is you.

Think of your triangle as a target, and aim for the middle with the work you do. Keep in mind, it's okay if you don't hit the center of this target, as long as you don't hit entirely outside it.

Now come up with three companies or individuals that will help you aim. For example, a few years ago when Julien first did this exercise, the three individuals who helped keep him on target were Marshall McLuhan, Seth Godin, and Tony Robbins. When he told Chris about the exercise, Chris chose Sir Richard Branson, Lady Gaga, and Howard Stern. (Our choices would be different now, but the point remains the same.)

Now, every time you have a message to articulate, you can remain on target by thinking of your triangle. Are you aiming in the right direction? Is the message written the right way? Or, if you consistently aim outside your target, consider changing your core three.

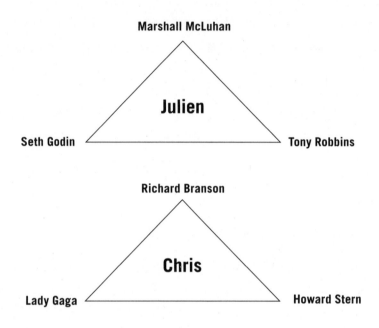

Method 2: Emotion + Information

This second method is interesting too, but totally different. Do any of these, or all of them if you have the time. Then repeat them a few years later and see how much things have changed.

After you have worked on a few key ideas, consider what the principal information is within them. Usually this can be done by category (social media, business, relationships, etc.). Draw these as circles and see how they overlap, perhaps with a Venn diagram. If you can come up with only one (if, say, you're all about coffee), then try to distill it into many messages (fair trade, etc.).

Okay, once you have a few of those, think of a few emotions you display them *with*. This will make you realize that you need to present your ideas with an emotion, or they'll lack Echo (another Impact Attribute we'll discuss later). If you're displaying only information, others simply won't connect well with it.

One example of this would be the way that Julien wrote *The Flinch*. People often say it's written as if by a drill sergeant. What this means is that it's the information for self-growth alongside the emotion of anger with a smidgen of hope. You'll notice that combining the information with feelings like sadness and remorse delivers a whole other message for a totally different audience.

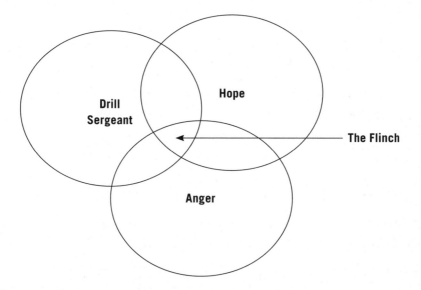

Try this out now with your project. If you are delivering a certain message, or if you're not getting the type of customers you want, ask yourself what emotion you're placing alongside your message. Is it congruent with whom you want to attract?

Method 3: Being the X of Y

Julien once spent a whole conference (three days or so) helping people clarify their identities and the way they introduced themselves. He came across a great tactic that helped almost every single person figure out who they were, whether as an individual, a small firm, or a start-up. The method is deceptively simple but very effective. Here it is.

Begin with a single character, usually (but not necessarily) fictional. It can be a cartoon character known for a specific thing (say, Captain Planet) or a real-life historical figure (like Ulysses S. Grant). It should always be a well-known name but never what we would call an A-list name (such as James Bond), because that sounds like bragging. Choose someone you admire or look up to.

Then decide what industry you would like to be part of. Political bloggers, MBAs, and others will each have their own answer to this question. Whatever industry you choose, make sure it's where you want to work or a place where other people would like to be, because this method is about catching people's interest.

Then, combine the two into "the X of Y." Simple.

The result of this exercise is almost always a self-definition that is more interesting than what you previously had. For example, one *Harvard Business Review* writer became the MacGyver of innovation. (She puts small, distinct pieces together into a much better whole.) You yourself could become the Aquaman of globalization (bringing together two separate worlds (water and air) and helping them make sense together). But whatever it is you come up with, we guarantee it will be better than how you previously introduced yourself. Try it.

ARTICULATION: HOW TO RATE YOURSELF

How clear is your idea? This is an important section of the equation because you only get one chance to leave a strong impression. Consider it your elevator pitch. Will your one chance, right this instant, result in a clear impression in your target's head, or will you end up looking embarrassed trying to explain what you do or what your idea is?

Ideas no longer get second chances. We need to know how to express ourselves clearly the first time.

Now, we assume that other parts of your concept aren't hindering people from understanding your idea. For example, when someone says, "How is this different from all the other blogs about social media?" they're asking about Contrast, not clarity. In this example, they know what you do; they just think it's deeply boring (and they may be right).

So we want to focus here on the clarification of an idea—making people care not because they've never seen it before but because it sticks in their head instantly.

Give your complex idea a name. Simplicity is a key part of clarity, and if you can give an idea a name (Gladwell's *The Tipping Point* comes to mind), you capture the imagination much more quickly.

Acronyms: We actually try to resist this idea, because it seems contrived, but we'd be remiss if we didn't mention it, so here goes. The Impact Attributes are interesting, but placing them in an order that results in the CREATE acronym is a good example that helps make it memorable. We also used this technique when we reformulated the David Maister, Charles Green, and Robert Galford Trust Equation in our last book. So $T=C*R*I/S$ became $C*R*I/S = T$. Generally, ideas that use human mnemonic devices are more memorable and clear than almost any other ideas, because we are verbal creatures who learn based on narrative and story.

Tell a story: Any time you express a complex idea, this is one way to simplify it. We naturally learn through stories and metaphors, so expressing ideas with them is simple and effective. This is why those terrible "business parable" books sell so well; they express simple ideas through narrative. Whether the story is real or imagined is actually irrelevant (some say the story in Robert Kiyosaki's *Rich Dad Poor Dad* never happened, for example); what matters is whether it resonates emotionally with the reader. We'll return to these concepts later in our discussion of Echo, but for now, remember that proper Articulation of an idea keeps it memorable.

One great example of Articulation comes to us from Chrysler, which has, interestingly, relaunched the Fiat brand in the United States. The company capitalized on the marketplace reopened by the Mini Cooper, as well as on U.S. gas prices, and brought back a car that hadn't been viewed as anything particularly notable before. How does Chrysler articulate what you're buying into on its site?

It mentions "Italian style," "emotional design," "rational appeal," and a lot of personalization options. In a few short phrases, you get a sense of what Chrysler wants you to know about its car.

Swing over to the Mini site, and its language is about "incredible gas mileage," "premium technology," "legendary performance," and "smiling."

A car purchase is an interesting way to think about Articulation. It is an exercise in justification from start to finish. If you've gone without a car for a long while, you must justify why you now need to buy one again. If you've got an older but still functional car, you have to justify why you're upgrading or replacing it. Buying a sports car versus an economy car requires a story told to oneself, and then sometimes the rest of the family.

It gets interesting when a car's advertising must speak to the passionate reason why we're *really* buying the car while arming us with the information we'll need to make others in our decision-making circle (or only ourselves) feel good about the decision.

Both Fiat and Mini talk about how their cars are economical and fuel efficient, yet they both rave about their design and performance capabilities. They cover both bases, and each Web site's ad copy, by the way, does it with fewer than fourteen words.

We've talked about brevity a lot throughout the book, but its value can't be highlighted enough. In every case where you seek to get a point across, brevity is a core selling point. It will get you much further than trying to paint with words. You'll see.

IMPACT EXAMPLE: INSTAGRAM

On the day the news broke that social-networking giant Facebook was buying photo-sharing application Instagram for one billion dollars, opinions on why and what next were quite mixed. We were split in our opinions. Julien thought it was a great purchase and cited the thirty million acquired users, plus the revitalization of photo sharing, which had reportedly been dwindling on Facebook's own platform, never mind the fact that Facebook seemed genuinely threatened by Instagram's dominance of mobile photo sharing. Chris dug into some reporting that said Instagram might be an angle Facebook could use to break into China.[1] We decided to look at Instagram to see how it matched up against the Impact Equation.

Contrast: There are hundreds (thousands, actually!) of photo applications in the Apple and Android stores. Instagram, however, backed its app with a social network, so people could follow certain tags, certain photographers, and more. Tying an application to a network of like-minded people made for good Contrast, but it wasn't enough. Only

---

1 Source: http://blogs.wsj.com/chinarealtime/2012/04/10/will-instagram-help -facebook-crack-china/.

when the founders had made their third photo application, simplifying every time, did they get to something that had the Contrast it needed to win.

Reach: If Instagram really is the gateway drug to get Facebook into China, that's a great way to extend Reach. Even if that isn't the case, Facebook purchased thirty million passionate Instagram users and gave its photo-sharing credentials a powerful shot in the arm. Since they are leaving Instagram be, there is no question it will continue growing.

Exposure: Facebook's brand isn't mentioned at all inside of Instagram, but that doesn't matter. To the users who care, Instagram is a more highly valued brand, and every time a new, great picture appears, Instagram gets a shot of Exposure.

Articulation: Instagram is an almost perfectly simple application. Take, edit, and share photos. Photos, if you think about it, are a great currency for social networking. What do we like to share? We love sharing photos of our kids, our new cars, our whatever. The app's social network is simple to articulate too. It's not nearly as complex as Facebook or Google+. People who like sharing photos congregate there. Instagram gets high marks in Articulation.

Trust: Does Instagram have our Trust? It probably would rank higher in a survey than its new parent company. Facebook goes in and out of public favor with privacy issues and other conundrums that shake its users' comfort levels. Instagram? It has earned Trust over the last few years. It was a very big seller on Android's marketplace in its first few weeks on that platform, ranking number three overall at its zenith. That says something.

Echo: Do you see yourself in Instagram? This is a no-brainer. The application is built to let you take, edit, and share photos from your life. Chris's joke is that Instagram turns your otherwise boring life into album cover art. Instagram also earns Echo by mapping into all kinds of social networks besides Facebook, thus creating a bridge between the application and wherever your crowd is.

We rank Instagram as a highly successful user of the Impact Attributes. You might be lucky enough to have Facebook come and offer you a billion dollars for your company, but if not, think about how Instagram worked its Contrast and how it articulated the value of the product. You might not have thirty million users or customers, but you can certainly benefit from thinking about how adding some kind of user-to-user social experience might help your product grow.

It's early in the acquisition, but we think it will be a smooth integration and people will extend their use of photo-based networking and sharing even more with this product. A picture is worth a thousand words, they say, but evidently, it's also worth a billion dollars.

PART **3** **Platforms**

Ask a Los Angeles native about Angelyne, and they'll come up with many theories. Some say she's the wife of a billboard king, though none know who. Others remember her from some punk band in the eighties. But none of these theorists actually know the truth—or if they do, they're not telling.

Angelyne first popped up in the 1980s on posters throughout the city. She later began appearing on billboards, which became so famous in their own regard that they appeared in the backgrounds of movies like *Get Shorty*, *Volcano*, and *The Fan*.

If you see one, or find one on Google, you'll see her painted portrait, not a photograph in the traditional billboard style. Her appearance is a combination of *The Jetsons*-like style and Joan from *Mad Men*. The billboards were gigantic, monolithic renditions that viewers couldn't help but notice. They were fifty feet tall, for God's sake. Everyone saw them, even though no one knew who she was.

Angelyne really did exist—she had been seen about town—but what she did was a mystery. Was she a model, an actress, or a singer? It didn't seem to matter. Because she was on billboards, she was somebody . . . wasn't she?

Billboards are obviously expensive, but nobody knows exactly where the money for the billboards came from or why she chose to publicize her Bettie Page–type pictures on hundred-foot-high canvases throughout the city. As time went on, Angelyne began to become a celebrity in her own right—not for any specific talent, skill, or exceptional accomplishment, but for the simple fact that everyone knew her name.

Angelyne was among the first people in America to become "famous for being famous," like Paris Hilton and many others since. In other words, Angelyne is a testament to the power of platform.

Even now, years later, Angelyne still has a massive fan club—forty thousand people, they say—who pay a yearly fee for the privilege. Her platform has carried her throughout these years, much further than most celebrities or one-hit wonders last.

If billboards were enough to make Angelyne famous, is a powerful platform enough to put you on top? Well, maybe. If your platform is strong enough, you might fall into a kind of rich-get-richer scenario, that's true. But it's more complex than that, because you can't just expect an amazing platform to be given to you. There is no record deal waiting for you, no movie producer tapping you on the shoulder in the checkout line, and definitely no one with billboards just waiting to put your face on them.

Our story necessarily began with ideas, because without those ideas, you are nothing. But our work has to continue, because one story or idea, no matter how perfect, will never be enough. The next step is to build your own transmitter, your own newspaper, or your own TV station. That is what platform is all about.

Not too long ago, the expression was "Never argue with a man who buys ink by the barrel." Thankfully, now ink is cheap. Anyone can have that power, including you. All you need is a blueprint.

#

A powerful platform does not appear on its own. Instead, it must be built, and that is more about what happens outside the platform than inside. This is true no matter the platform, whether it exists virtually or in real life.

Let's say you want to start a conference—an event at which dog lovers, say, gather together to talk about all things dogs. Thousands of these events probably exist everywhere, but no matter; we're going to assume the first one is about to be invented.

So you come up with the logistics for this event. It will happen on a weekend in November, you decide, and it will happen in a convention hall in your hometown. Tickets cost twenty dollars if you're an early bird or twenty-five if you show up at the door. So far, so good. Next you want to bring people together for the event.

Okay, here comes the question. Do you

a. go out to dog parks, talk to pet owners, put up fliers on your favorite pet site; or

b. go to the middle of your now-rented convention center and start shouting into the void, hoping dog owners will hear you?

Right. Exactly.

All platforms, from Twitter to Google+ to in-person networks to speaking events and more, require outside work. They cannot be built from the inside out. They must occur from the outside in, building from one platform to another.

Picture this, but now on Twitter. You create an account and add a nice picture and custom background. You begin tweeting amazing stuff, but unfortunately, no one is there to hear it.

If this is happening to you, and you are waiting for someone to come across your channel and tweet about it, creating a barrage of interest and fans, you are wasting your time and may be delusional.

It is extremely unlikely that a single person will (a) come across your channel, (b) find something they consider interesting, (c) find it so interesting that they decide to spread it among the people they care about, and (d) have significant influence. In other words, you have better chances of winning the lottery.

Therefore, our focus in this section is to leave you with a practical guide to building a channel that has significant audience, so you may take advantage of the channel building that others have done and finally get a significant platform of your own.

What We Mean by "Platform"

There are lots of definitions for "platform." We're talking about the combination of tools you use to reach others and communicate ideas. In the traditional world, most people had very little access to platforms with any real kind of Reach. Mainstream media had television, radio, newspapers, and magazines. Meanwhile, individuals had telephones, letters, and the "opportunity" to run advertisements on various media channels. Web sites in the early days cost tens of thousands of dollars to make and maintain. My, how times have changed.

We now have access to inexpensive or free Web site creation. We all have access to a video-distribution channel (YouTube and hundreds of other similar platforms). We can build e-mail lists that rival the distribution of any mainstream newspaper. We can build social networks whose size dwarfs the populations of some cities. We can buy a video camera for under a hundred dollars and create our own "shows," if we're so inclined.

When we talk about platform, we mean the creation of some combination of the above. Even mainstream celebrities work in multimedia mode now. Kim Kardashian rose to fame with her reality TV show, but she greatly improved her platform by blogging regularly and actively using Twitter. Others have gone the opposite way.

Lucas Cruikshank, creator of the horribly annoying Fred Figglehorn character, started from scratch. He posted "Fred" videos on YouTube and rapidly grew a following. In fact, he was the first YouTube publisher to reach a million subscribers. Cruikshank parlayed this effort into a Fred movie made with Nickelodeon, a second movie, a TV series, and soon a third movie. (At this point, you should stop reading, go to YouTube, type in "Fred," and see who we're talking about.)

From zero, Cruikshank turned his YouTube platform into a large mainstream presence and many opportunities. We know you aren't likely to finish this book and start recording yourself speaking in a high-pitched, squeaky voice. And yet it's important to realize that this is exactly what brought millions of viewers, fame, and success (so far enduring success, at that) to one young man without access to traditional channels.

He's not alone. In her spare time, former assisted-living worker Amanda Hocking wrote seventeen supernatural-themed novels. She tried publishing them via the traditional route and received rejection after rejection. No one cared one bit for her romantic supernatural novels. So she decided to self-publish them on Amazon.

In no time, she was selling over nine thousand books a day. Yes, over nine thousand.

Amanda made over two million dollars in sales on her own, mostly by pricing the books so low that people felt no risk purchasing them. People came, then more people, and word of mouth pushed these books up the Amazon sales charts, which then spurred even more activity. Soon she was the game to beat.

And that's when St. Martin's Press gave her a book deal for two million dollars more.

Amanda started from zero. Now? Her platform is giant. She

blogs, tweets, uses Facebook, and stays well connected with her fans, who will buy her next mainstream books without question.

Don't discount this if you're a plumber or a business-to-business air conditioner vendor. You can have the same success. You can find the method to build a platform of value for your business. Our friend Marcus Sheridan did it with swimming pool sales and service. Our friend Joel Libava does it with his franchising consulting. We know many successful people who don't sell the sexiest product or service in the world and yet, they are very successful.

The point we're making here is that platform is a powerful part of impact and that you will have to work in earnest on this detail. We've divided platform into two chapters: Reach and Exposure, which you'll learn about next.

4 Reach

Okay, let's be frank: The real reason most people picked up this book isn't Trust, and it probably isn't Contrast either. Those are important parts of the equation, sure, and everyone wants them, but we suspect that what people are actually after is something a little bit more obvious, a little less "sniper rifle" and a little more "giant freaking laser beam." Does that make any sense?

Reach is what's coveted, because it often comes with a great deal of prestige. The girl with a hundred thousand Twitter followers has an amazing lead over the rest of the pack. It is also possible to practically *buy* Reach, as you can purchase Twitter followers, buy e-mail addresses to expand your list, or whatever else you might find interesting. Although these options exist, they are not truly Reach in the sense that we mean it here. These options are more like faking Reach temporarily.

Let's put it this way: We heard a story one time about a guy who finds other people's ATM receipts. He picks up all the receipts showing big bank balances. He keeps them. Then he attempts to show them to girls in order to create interest. Well, faking Reach is kind of like that. It might work sometimes, but the charade is often quickly revealed and the interest, if any, does not last long. So faking your Reach may work for a while, but it doesn't actually expand anything. In order to obtain and truly expand your Reach, you need to work extremely hard. You also need to be a little more direct than most.

Reach is almost never built quickly. A musician can tour the country over several years and still not convince a hundred thousand people to buy a record. More likely, our buddy builds true fans one at a time, convincing perhaps one person per show and convincing another after that. The process is painstaking but powerful, because it also involves practice and makes you a master. It's how Louis C.K. became one of the best-known comedians in the world—not quickly but over fifteen years—one YouTube view at a time. This is what true Reach is like. It takes time, but it stays with you.

We'll help guide you up the mountain.

#

Chris is friends with world-renowned author Paulo Coelho. His work has been translated into more than seventy languages and published in over 170 countries. He even has a world record for this kind of distribution. A handful of months back, Chris was watching a clip of U.S. president Barack Obama talking about something, and then and there, the president quoted Coelho's most famous work, *The Alchemist*.

And yet Coelho, like many of us, is still in need of a robust platform with lots of Reach.

Why? Because ideas without Reach are like plants without sunlight. They dry up and shrivel and sink back into the soil. Even the best ideas, if forgotten, lack power. Like all living things, ideas thrive on Reach.

The Alchemist is actually a story about Reach and impact. It was written as a kind of parable after Coelho completed the five-hundred-mile Road of Santiago de Compostela pilgrimage (which Julien has also completed, incidentally). In the book, a young shepherd leaves the place he knows to go off in search of treasure and learns the language of the world along the way.

In each encounter, the boy finds someone who is missing something. Sometimes the problem is that people lack the vision to create an idea with the right shape. Some people have ideas but haven't worked on their platform and Reach. Others haven't quite figured out how their story echoes, so they get lost in their own little worlds.

But if someone is famous enough to attain world records for being so widely distributed and translated and is so famous as to have the president of the United States quote him during a speech, shouldn't that be enough amplification to attain Reach? What's missing? Well, a real platform.

First, it's interesting to consider that the big ideas and messages in Coelho's works are widely known by other people of merit and status. Coelho speaks to diverse groups like the United Nations and prominent people from all over. But that doesn't mean he has the attention of "the people at large," as it were. Why? Because these leaders of higher status and standing tend to congregate among themselves, and though they have absorbed the messages of Coelho's works (those who are lucky enough to have read them), those ideas don't always disseminate "down" (and we're not using this word in judgment but rather to suggest that there is still a hierarchy in play) to others in their organizations.

The fabled "grass roots" do indeed have some value here. Let's switch entirely from world-shaping messages inside a book first published in 1988 to the land of YouTube, circa 2011, realize that Rebecca Black's "Friday" video, like it or hate it, had over 167 million views in a handful of months, and it continues to spread. This should be a "needle off the record" moment.

Did we really just contrast Paulo Coelho with Rebecca Black? Yes, we did. And we'll compare him to deadmau5 (a famous music producer, pronounced "dead mouse") later. Oh, that Paulo Coelho. He travels in unique circles.

A book, even a book that shows up in the Kindle or Nook store, requires a lot of push to be distributed. First, it costs money. Second, one must read and absorb it. Third, the shareability of a book is fairly limited (nearly nil in the digital format without piracy, and only by hand in the physical world).

By comparison, Rebecca Black's video can be shared with one mouse click. Take a little extra time and you can blast it across several social networks and earn her millions more eyeballs. Even if you saw it early on, some several thousand people will encounter it today, form their own opinion (often negative), and share it (in appreciation or disgust, or just to stick that song in someone else's ear for a while).

Reach can be a very tricky thing to accomplish.

Comparing these two experiences is a great way to talk about popularity, stardom, success, and fame versus impact. Do you think Rebecca Black has the same level of access to world leaders as Paulo Coelho? Not even a little bit. Do you think that Black will contribute a body of work that spans three decades (and hopefully many more)? It's not likely. Will we easily remember her name and legacy in a few years? That's to be decided.

Which one will get invited onto a late-night TV show this year, though? Black. Which one will be able to span other people's platforms and gain even more access and Reach? Black.

Is Reach fair? No. Did we ever, ever, *ever* mention "fair" in this entire book? No. Nor will we. "Fair" is a lie that the vanquished tell one another while licking their wounds. There's nothing fair about Reach.

To keep Reach alive and drive impact, Echo and Articulation

must be considered in similar measure. In this case, Echo is about keeping the message alive and trying to tailor it to modern surroundings. The story of *The Alchemist* is as old as time, and yet it's a message that resonates with people today. But how will it reach a new generation?

What if there were retellings that cast the story in modern parables? What if twelve contemporary authors told their own small bite of the story in their own unique voice? What if Paulo Coelho went beyond the written word and into video? Maybe your smart phone needs an *Alchemist* app to keep you living the message?

Echo is keeping the message fresh so it feels pertinent to newcomers. People have an unfair "not new enough" bias, it seems, so when we see something that's a year older than our discovery of it, it's believed to be no longer relevant.

Articulation means keeping the message brief and bite size. *The Alchemist* isn't very long even by modern book-length standards, but we live in a world that seems to have trouble with more than 140 characters at a time. With more and more people receiving hundreds of e-mails a day and fewer people reading for leisure than ever before, giving people a "sample" or a "tapas" version of *The Alchemist* would give Coelho a chance to lure a new audience (and build more Reach) into the clutches of his world-changing ideas. But would it be worth it?

Don't weep for Paulo Coelho. He has (at the time of this writing) 7.2 million fans on Facebook and three million followers on Twitter, and he amassed over eighty thousand followers in the *first three weeks* after signing up for Google+. He has an impressive and active platform of loving admirers. And yet it's clear that to accomplish his goal of changing the world, he needs more.

Oh, and if you haven't read *The Alchemist*, pick it up. It may change your life.

Why Platform Is Essential to Audience Capture

Since the beginning of time, merchants of widgets and ideas have been trying to get people interested in what they're selling. They use a variety of strategies—advertising, word of mouth, getting on top of a box and barking into a crowded square, and more. They've tried everything. Some methods have worked, while others, not so much. Yet every single day, new people attempt to sell their ideas through a variety of ineffective methods. They are reinventing the wheel when they should see what has worked for others and iterate from that instead.

Looking at advertising is one of the best ways to understand this. The TV-industrial complex is slowly being dismantled. Advertising is not as effective as it once was, yet new business owners continue to focus on it to draw attention to their new business. Sometimes they do worse and think that they absolutely *need* a storefront in order to be seen. In other words, they think of what they know. It's a natural reaction, although an ineffective one. This is the same reason the average person is more afraid of a shark attack than a traffic accident—because it is more vivid and real in their mind, even though traffic accidents happen much more frequently and are just as horrible.

So the most common methods of obtaining visibility are in fact the least effective. They are by definition most crowded, since they are the business owner's first thought, so the market for attention in these spaces gets competitive first. But for us, competition means death. Instead, we need a place where we are top of mind as often as possible. Building a platform for yourself satisfies this need. Having a platform on the Web, accessible to all, satisfies it best.

Platform is the second part of our structure—perhaps the most important part, since literally anyone with enough Reach can contact and influence a group large enough to have a significant impact on society. This is also the most important part of the structure to disrupt, since the hegemony of platform owners from before the Internet age led to a disproportionately small segment of the population having too significant an influence on the rest.

In other words, they've told us what to do for long enough. Now it's our turn.

The power of the platform in the twenty-first century is that it can reach anyone, at any time, in any place. Platform was one of the decisive factors of the 2008 U.S. presidential election, in which Barack Obama's connection to his constituents through modern platforms allowed for quick mobilization in time of need. It will be even more significant in 2012, as this book is published, because it is easier and more effective than ever to reach people directly (their mobile phones being a prominent method).

This same phenomenon is available to anyone—once a significant audience is built, it facilitates almost any goal you have. The increased network that comes with a huge platform will help you get things done faster. Network can be transferred from one goal to another, helping you shift careers if you want to, or get advantages and information that others simply can't have. In other words, platform multiplies power. The more vast and more effective it is, the stronger you become.

There will come a time when everyone will have a significant platform—that time, in fact, is already coming about. We see people spreading messages more quickly than ever before through Facebook accounts, helping a media democracy emerge, one that could never before have existed due to the cost of developing a platform and distributing ideas.

We hope to convince you that developing a platform is the most effective method for keeping your business afloat during good times and bad. We hope to make it clear that, at any point, your most effective job-search tool will be something like your blog or

Google+ account. It may even be one of the most effective means of finding a spouse. But perhaps we're getting ahead of ourselves.

Your marital status notwithstanding, platform is important because, without it, you are far too dependent on other people's delivery methods. There is, we will argue, a massive difference between building a platform and being dependent on others' Reach—a phenomenon we'll call "hype," or perhaps you'll recognize it by its more traditional name, "advertising."

Advertising means borrowing audience attention and diverting it toward what you're trying to sell. Whether in newspapers, television, or banner ads, traditional advertising usually distracts people from their interest and toward something else. But platform doesn't do this—platform is different.

The platform is the channel itself. When people gather around a television to watch the most recent episode of *Mad Men*, they are there to pay attention to the show, not the advertising between the segments. (We are conscious, incidentally, of the irony of our use of a show about advertising as our example.) Advertising distracts. It's when people go to the bathroom or make a phone call. They don't do this during the television program itself because the show is why they're there.

This is why platform is important—it is not a diversion from the audience's interests. Those who care about cars will focus on the car channel and ignore the hype in between. Those who enjoy the fashion channel will, likewise, ignore the advertising between pieces of content, with one exception: If the focus of the advertising matters to them too, then the hype has a chance. But in most cases advertising fails, and besides, platform is more effective, is more profitable, and works better over the long term, and finally, you have more control over it.

Platform may soon be essential for a successful business. Let's get ahead of the game and understand how it works.

Creating Content with a Purpose

The new platform's purpose is audience building. It's fair to say that, if you're sitting here right now, even with a great idea, the likelihood of influencing a significant portion of the population is slim. Therefore, we need to reach people—a significant enough mass that we can create an income stream from it or enough to influence a normally unreachable group of people.

So a new platform is like a new business or even a person in a new city—it should always be attempting to reach out to new individuals and place them inside its network. Doing so expands Reach exponentially. It's not only effective, though—it's also among the easiest things to do.

Reaching people does nothing unless you provide them with enough value to make them stop what they're doing, either now or later, and participate in your media. So a blog post must be well written enough or compel with its story enough that it will cause the reader to think

a. this is an interesting new voice;

b. I've been thinking this forever; finally someone is saying it; or

c. I've never thought about this before!

The most significant absence from this list is the reader's reaction to an attempt to convert him into a customer, get him to pay for information, or extract value from him in some other way. You are not at this stage yet—what Tim O'Reilly might call the "contraction" stage—you are at the expansion stage, and expansion demands free because free reduces friction to near zero.

How long does this stage last, you may ask yourself? After all, you can't be capturing audience forever, building and building until you can no longer pay your mortgage or have any new ideas. Well, as usual, our answer is "It depends." But it's also "It lasts as long as possible."

In other words, the more you delay the process of extracting value from your network and channels, the faster you will build audience and goodwill. Then goodwill and value can be extracted more effectively later on, when it matters.

The Value Capture

Where many people run into difficulty in their pursuit of impact is in understanding how and when to extract value from their platform. Remember that "value" doesn't always mean money. It might mean access. It might mean social proof. It might mean something else. And then again, "value" does also sometimes mean money.

Understanding how and when to extract value is an important piece of the Impact Equation that many others have missed. Don't judge yourself too harshly if you've tried and failed in the past. Many of us have. Here's a quick story.

Years ago, the comedian Ricky Gervais had the most popular audio podcast in the world. He had more downloads than any other podcast by far. He had a vast and enviable platform. At this point, Gervais decided it was time to extract value (and who knows, maybe some manager somewhere advised him on this). He decided to change his model and charge for podcasts. With such a large and loving audience, with so many new subscribers every week, he felt sure that by asking for just a small amount of money from so many people, he would win big.

The moment Gervais (or his people) turned on the pay gate to his content was the moment he fell from the number one spot in the iTunes podcast chart to the number who-remembers spot. He made a small amount of money on the first paid downloads, but it dwindled to nothing almost immediately. Of course, when he switched back to free later, the crowds didn't exactly rush back in to resume their passion and commitment.

What else might Gervais have done? He might have gone the route of another funny guy, Adam Carolla. Adam's podcast has risen more recently, and he went with the more traditional route of seeking sponsors who want access to his audience. He extracts value from the sponsors, so that his audience doesn't have to pay. This results in more satisfaction all the way around, even though it's the traditional method.

Now, Gervais wasn't wrong for seeking money from his audience. That's the public radio model, by the way; more than 50 percent of public radio stations' revenue comes from individual contributors instead of sponsors or underwriters. It just didn't fit the reality of the landscape. Podcasts are a new and difficult-to-navigate platform, with far more choices for consumption, so Gervais didn't have the right environment for his effort to extract value.

Thoughts on Value and Sources

The value of a large platform depends partly on whether that platform will take an action based on your recommendation. If you're Oprah, and you recommend a book to read, that book sells far more than other books on the shelf. If you're Chris Brogan, and you ask your followers to give twenty dollars to a charity to help hungry children, you'll hit your goal because the audience feels that you give value to them. Another way to extract value from a large platform is to offer advertising to people who might want to reach that community. You can also extract nonfinancial value by, for instance, requesting participation in projects. But this all assumes a large platform.

The value of a smaller platform might be a tighter-knit community. For instance, if you're Sermo, you've got a small group of medical professionals that allows for different value. If you're Vistage, you lead a peer-leadership group, mostly for CEOs, that caters to a smaller set than, say, businesspeople at large. With that change in size comes an opportunity for even more value. If we forget the premium accounts, the price of having a LinkedIn account is zero dollars. The price to be a member of Vistage is thousands of dollars a year. Vistage extracts more value from a smaller and more distinct set of interactions than LinkedIn does from smaller bites of revenue from a larger set of people.

When to Extract Value

Some people worry that "immediately" is the wrong time to extract value. That's not especially true. It's more a matter of context. If you set the stage for a product or service that costs money, for instance, you might have an introductory rate first, but realize that charging someone more later might cause a problem. People get used to the status quo: If something is free, they don't intend to pay. If something costs one rate, they don't expect a rise in price. Unless . . .

And "unless" is a lovely word, isn't it?

Look at the auto industry. Honda, Volkswagen, Toyota, and many other non-U.S. automakers entered the U.S. market by offering a low-cost product that led U.S. buyers to consider a switch based on price. Then they released more expensive products that appeared as "improved quality" and "luxury." That's another method to consider.

However, look at the difference between what Gervais did and what Honda did. Gervais didn't offer a "deluxe" podcast. He merely offered the same podcast, now with a price. See the difference?

Value could be a whole book unto itself. Know this: If you give away as much as you can for free and charge for only the most difficult parts, you will corner both parts of a new value model that improves your impact. It's how we do what we do, and it has served us well as a model.

Little Bloggers Grow Up

We talked about this in *Trust Agents*. The saying "Little bloggers grow up" comes from speaker and provocateur Liz Strauss. The notion is that we should be kind to the up-and-comers in our world, because we never know where they'll go next. We both subscribe to this concept and prescribe it to people looking to build platform.

One way to build a platform from nothing is to find the other up-and-comers and build community among them. Comment on their posts. Interact with them on their social networks. If others in your larger space are also trying to build platform, a little bit of sharing and cross-promoting goes a long way. For instance, if you're a real estate professional in Spokane, Washington, it doesn't hurt you to promote posts and ideas from people in Eugene, Oregon, or Doncaster in the UK, but it can benefit you. The more you promote others' good work, the more they'll be inclined to share your work when the timing makes sense.

Another way to build platform is to give back to others who are learning. If your profession has a college or professional school supporting it, you might meet with educators who teach courses you could add value to and offer to talk with them, either in person or via Skype. Chris talks with college marketing and PR classes twice or more a month, mostly because it's a way to share and give back but also because all those students will eventually graduate and find their way into large companies and positions of power. It sure helps to have left a positive personal impression on them, should future opportunities arise.

There's a balancing act to growing platform. We've talked about promoting the up-and-comers and giving back to students (they're up-and-comers from a different angle), but you also have to connect with people who might be a little larger in your industry. One strategy is to offer guest posts to bloggers in your space with larger audiences. (Before you discount the idea that there are bloggers already talking about your space, swing by alltop.com and see if you can find people writing about your industry.)

If you want to go that route, it's good to comment and be part of that person's community before you offer to write a guest post. People with larger platforms often have many people offering to "help" by writing guest material, and they often have to turn away a lot of newcomers simply because there are so many offers. The way to get *your* offer accepted is to become known and feel like you're part of the blogger's community. How? Comment often on that person's posts. Respond to that person's tweets or other social media. It's the same as with the up-and-comers. The goal is just a bit different.

\#

One of Chris's biggest inspirations in business is Sir Richard Branson of Virgin fame. He has followed Branson's work and books for years and years. Imagine Chris's delight, then, years into his own business journey, when he got the opportunity to speak with and interview Sir Richard for a feature magazine article. Next up: Chris intends to leverage that experience to meet more of his heroes and to potentially meet Branson in person.

In his book *Screw Business as Usual*, Branson name-drops everyone from the Dalai Lama to Bill Clinton. But he started with a self-published student magazine at sixteen and had no real reason to have access to anyone. Yet he is now a global force to be reckoned with. This kind of access doesn't come from nowhere.

Our first book deal came because we had a platform and a built-in audience. This book is the result of that one and the fact that it hit the *New York Times* best-seller list. That book led to access. If you read the blurbs on the back, there are some of the "usual suspects" of business and marketing books, but there's also the former CEO of General Motors, Fritz Henderson. That came from building a platform and using it to obtain access.

Access with Purpose

It's important to note that when we gain access to influential people, we never come with an "ask" in mind. Instead, we aim to serve and be helpful. When Chris approached Sir Richard Branson, it was with the goal of landing a cover story for a major magazine in support of Branson's new book. That this also satisfied Chris's dream of connecting with a legend was secondary to the service provided.

In almost every case, the purpose of our outreach to someone influential has been first and foremost to help them. The side benefit is the social proof that clearly we have something of value to offer, because we are afforded time by people of standing.

But again, let us stress: It's important that you connect with people to serve them first. This delivers the best value and impact for everyone involved. Coming to someone with your hand out for help is always far less attractive than creating something of value for the person you're hoping to connect with.

Leverage Your Platform

As you develop your media platform and build a way to communicate to more and more people (or to the right people), use it to attract people who have something to share. Everyone in the universe is seeking more attention for his or her project or cause and aching to tell even more people about it. Sure, sometimes people are so oversaturated with requests for their time that they have to pick and choose their media venues. Do what you can to make yours seem like the best possible place for the job.

The most common way to achieve this is to publish interviews to your blog or Web site. One challenge, however, is learning to do an interview that shows off the guest in his or her best light and is of value to your community. It's very important to practice.

One quick side note or homework assignment about this advice. The best way to learn how to interview better is to experience the work of great interviewers. Look at how Larry King did what he did. See how David Letterman does it. Observe Tom Chiarella's great interviews in print. Learn by dissecting the questions others have asked and seeing how you could adapt them for your own interests. Experiment and be willing to be bold. Oh, and a bonus piece of advice: Never start with "How did you get started?" It's the sign of an amateur.

Use your "wins" to gain more access. Once you interview Bob Iger, Tony Robbins, and Sir Richard Branson, doors open to others. Where do you start? Reach as high as you can, and start there. (Again, always do this in service of the other person before your own goals and needs. This can get really scammy and social-ladder-climbing really quickly otherwise.)

Let's talk about what this Exposure can do for you and those you help along the way.

About TED

Okay, no discussion of platform would be complete without at least a little examination of what has become perhaps one of the most famous platforms on the Web today, that is to say, the TED conference.

TED, for most, needs no introduction. It is a world-class event attended by U.S. presidents, billionaire CEOs, as well as some of the most insightful and inspirational artists and scientists of our time (not to mention at least one of the authors of this book, who managed to sneak in somehow). Occurring once a year, in Long Beach, California, it has also spawned a number of side events, such as TEDGlobal and TEDAfrica, not to mention the hundreds of independently organized events, branded TEDx, that have been launched by universities and communities around the globe. Since its first event in 1984, TED has truly become a global brand that represents both excellence in idea design and collective purpose.

But there is more to it than that, at least the way we think of it. Though TED is an event that has reached millions of viewers and touched many people, it is also the perfect example of platform because the organizers themselves do not generate the presentations at all but simply borrow and curate them. This is an important distinction, because it means that they can focus on the platform, and only the platform, ensuring it is among the best in the world.

There is something at work here that is worth dissecting. While it's true that most conferences do not design presentations, other events have not come close to representing what TED does. TED's motto is "ideas worth spreading," yet TED itself does not create these ideas; it simply recognizes them and gives them a platform from which to be heard.

All the best platforms are like this: the *Huffington Post*, the best-known global magazines, and more. They are aggregators. They focus on what they do best—obtaining Reach and, through Reach, increasing Exposure—while letting another team address the very thing that makes TED great: world-class content.

Yet the two cannot be separated. Without great content, the platform is useless and becomes barren and abandoned. Without the platform, the great idea is invisible and unheard amid the cacophony of the idea marketplace.

What can we learn from TED about platform? Some of the conference's characteristics are surely coincidental and need not be emulated, but others are in fact critical to the platform's success, and we need to separate the former from the latter to ensure that we derive the right lessons. Here's how we see it. See if you agree with our conclusions.

A great platform means great access. If you develop a powerful platform, it becomes a brand in its own right. People become enamored of the brand and will be happy to participate based on the brand's positive connotations (see Echo in chapter 7). We saw this happen a few years ago with the *Huffington Post*—a quality that has since diminished because it feels like anyone can write there.

A great platform is exclusive. This is also part of access, because exclusivity by definition keeps the people on the inside feeling like they are having a unique experience. Another event, Summit Series, has developed a reputation for accepting only twenty-five-year-old millionaires as its attendees and speakers. This isn't true (at all), but the image does make people feel curious enough to want to see for themselves. And if you were accepted to this event, or invited to speak at it, you have to admit a part of you couldn't help but feel pleased.

A good platform should make you feel privileged to be involved, and this usually has to do with its attendees. Curating the experience means bringing in the right people, which, strangely enough, also restricts the Reach you can grow through it . . . at least at the beginning.

A great platform produces almost exclusively great content. If your content isn't excellent, your brand will not be either. TechCrunch, which sold to AOL last year for about forty million, was the exclusive, go-to source for all tech news and gossip. Because of its network, anything that happened in technology was published there first, helping keep exclusivity as well.

#

The best platforms are also like a rap supergroup. They enable the audience and fans of each individual to come together and appreciate the whole. If Will.i.am of the Black Eyed Peas comes together with Jennifer Lopez and Mick Jagger (as they did for "T.H.E." in December 2011), then the Mick Jagger fans become more aware of Jennifer Lopez and Will.i.am, and likewise across all members of the group.

Seth Godin did this after his book *Purple Cow* was released with a follow-up called *The Big Moo*. Collaborating with a group of authors including Malcolm Gladwell, Mark Cuban, Tom Peters, and more (together the "Group of 33"), Godin created a collaborative work that draws upon the prestige and audience of each in order to help carry all of them to a larger set of eyeballs.

We could learn a lot from TED, the Group of 33, even Jay-Z and Kanye West. They understand audience building in a way that seems to be lacking on the Web, where most channels are created by individuals and stay with them, and where the stars stand alone in their platform-building attempts. We need to see that piggybacking off other channels is naturally the most efficient way of working your way upward and that when at the top, we need to carry the up-and-comers as well.

How to Do a Launch

Musicians, conferences, and book authors are also different because they understand the concept of the launch. They don't publish every day; they publish once a month—or maybe even once a year—so they know they have to make a big splash and do it right.

Let's face it: Launch days are important. Maybe you have a new book or product, or you're changing the price of something old but interesting. You're going to want a big splash, like a huge ad campaign used to make when you put it in the *New York Times* or *Life* magazine or whatever other thing used to be important.

Well, this is the twenty-first century. Now you don't need those guys or any other major institution to give you a helping hand. Don't get us wrong; they give a boost, of course. But they are by no means necessary to the successful spread of information. For that, you don't need a huge newspaper, a television or radio station, or anything else. You just need a bunch of friends who have used the information in this book wisely.

Every single person who uses the tools we've written about here will be able to build a little bit of an audience that is slightly different from any other, no matter how similar the topic they both speak about. If your friend is writing about being a mom, and you are too, you will gather similar but distinct audiences based on your personalities, what you share, and how much work you put in. So you can use this magic to help any launch you end up doing. It doesn't matter how small or massive it may be; this strategy can scale, so you can use it anywhere.

1. Do not focus on your audience; focus on other audiences. The reason for this is simple: Your audience is already sold on you, which is why they follow and pay attention to you. Every piece of content you create (hopefully) sells them fur-

ther on who you are and what you do, so you don't need to work that hard at convincing them. Instead, work on collecting allies.

You collect allies in a number of different ways, but the most important part is just to make friends. Attend lots of different events, local and not; if you go to them with guns blazing, it's money well spent. Write guest posts for bloggers beforehand, or just e-mail someone to tell them you respect their work. Connect with people mercilessly and find a group whose ideas and messages resonate with what you're trying to deliver. Make a list of them—a big one.

2. Always ask beforehand, not the day of the actual launch. Everyone is busy. Even if you have built something that people care about in a big way, their own lives will always take center stage. So work with people up to a month in advance in order to push something on a predetermined day. Ask them if they'd like quotes, things to tweet, or interviews. If it connects with their audience, be forward about that and tell them you think you have a match. You'd be surprised how often people agree. After all, bloggers are the new journalists—their business thrives off good content, and if you have some, it will be evident to them.

3. Create real incentive and/or scarcity. What are people buying on your launch day? Is it your ideas, your attention, or the ability to better serve their own clients or help their own families? Amplify this feeling if that's the case by creating different incentives for those people who are in your or your neighbors' audiences.

Chris did this amazingly well (that's what Julien thinks, anyway) when he launched his book about Google+ in

December 2011, not only selling the book itself and the knowledge it contained (a serious steal at around ten bucks) but also offering a free webinar about how to publish a book for those who bought on a certain day. This moved the book up the Amazon rankings spectacularly fast, even for someone with Chris's high profile. He accomplished this by asking himself what his audience really valued besides the obvious social-media advice and realizing that much of his audience was also interested in book publishing. (Seriously, it's becoming all the rage. Everyone is doing it.) So this "extra," a simple add-on for Chris that was easy to make, was really valuable to his audience and pushed many of them off the fence and into buying territory.

4. The quality of your work must be consistently excellent. The best advertisement for your launch is the set of customers who have already bought from you and talked about it.

REACH: HOW TO RATE YOURSELF

Reach is perhaps the easiest of the attributes to measure. It's easy to compare, for example, how many subscribers, Twitter followers, Facebook fans, or whatever else you have against someone else. At the same time, it's very easy to get discouraged by looking at others' Reach. You see one guy in our industry with a huge audience, and you're not doing not so well. But all is not lost.

There are tons of factors that accelerate Reach, but one of the things we tend not to consider is how long a certain channel has been in place. So we take that into account before we get depressed about how few people we can reach.

For example, we could look at the Web site ZenHabits.net, run by our friend Leo Babauta, and compare it to another minimalist blog, TheMinimalists.com, run by our buddies Josh Millburn and Ryan Nicodemus. In absolute numbers, Zen Habits is winning with its 250,000 subscribers. It's also been around since January 2007 and has, by far, the most readers of any blog of its type. By contrast, The Minimalists has been around only sixteen months and has 12,000 readers. In absolute numbers, this is a daunting gap, and yet looking at how long each has been around shows a whole other game. Yet another method of checking this would be to see how many subscribers each blog has per post. There are different ways of comparing two channels.

Another reason to take it easy on Reach is that this attribute doesn't follow a linear curve. Instead, it accelerates over time. In other words, one reader can only tell so many people about something they like, but ten thousand can tell many more. So as time goes on, the same ideas can go further.

Chris often says that it took eight years for his Web site to get its first hundred readers. For Julien, it's about the same. Reach can get depressing if you look backward. So instead look forward and work hard to improve it.

IMPACT EXAMPLE: THE DOLLAR SHAVE CLUB

It wouldn't be an overstatement to say that Chris and Julien are infatuated with DollarShaveClub.com. The site and its business model are simple: Pick which kind of razor you want (from three different types), and pay a monthly subscription to receive blades for as long as you're a member.

What makes this interesting is that it is a simple model that will (a) make the owners a lot of money and (b) likely get Gillette (the company's biggest competitor) to buy it or at least emulate it. What might make this interesting to you is that Dollar Shave Club has every single element of the Impact Equation in spades. Let's look it over.

The site is simple. It features a two-minute video explaining (in comical format) what you get when you join Dollar Shave Club. Everything else is built to convert you into a subscriber.

You choose among three razors, pay, and never have to remember to buy razors again. It's simple. It's also ridiculously lucrative. Michael Dubin and partner Mark Levine won't give out numbers, but they started the company with $45,000 of their own money and have acquired tens of thousands of customers since their launch. If you assume an average of $5 a month per customer and twenty thousand customers a month, that's $100,000 a month. The cost of operating this business is obviously low. Its viral video cost $4,500 to make. We'd say this is a success.

Let's run it through the Impact Equation.

Contrast: The Dollar Shave Club sells just three types of blades, and none has any tech fancier than an aloe vera–lubricated strip. Its competitor, Gillette, has light-up, vibrating handles on its blades and celebrity endorsements. With the video endorsement on the front page ("Are our blades any good? No. OUR BLADES ARE F**KING GREAT"), Dollar Shave Club's blades sell themselves.

Reach: Dollar Shave Club's YouTube video received three million views in the first week. It was covered by all the major U.S. business media, plus the tech media, plus social-networking sites.

Exposure: Dollar Shave Club sends a subscriber a new blade in the mail every single month, and that new blade translates to a great shave, exposing the subscriber again and again to the magic of the brand. Each Exposure leads to a repeat reminder of the benefit of the service.

Articulation: You can't get much simpler than one dollar for two

blades, five dollars for four, and nine dollars for six. That's pretty simple stuff. Clarity is ten out of ten as far as we're concerned.

Trust: Here's one where Dollar Shave Club lags. People don't know
the brand. They don't know the CEO. They don't have much to go on.
But Dollar Shave Club has challenged Gillette by asking why you, the
customer, pay more so that Gillette can pay for celebrity endorsements. So in a way, it has poked a hole in the trustworthiness of its
main competitor, raising its own brand's Trust in the process.

Echo: Everything about the video and the Dollar Shave Club Web
site is built to make you feel like you're part of the joke. You're hip and
cool, and it's a "thing" for you to be part of Dollar Shave Club. We
haven't (yet) heard this mentioned at a party as any kind of status
symbol, but we believe it's not too far off.

Though the business exists solely on the Internet, and its marketing success came from a YouTube video, the business itself is plain,
old-fashioned product sourcing, distribution, and fulfillment. There's
nothing high tech. It's not sexy. It's a commodity. And yet Dollar
Shave Club is playing hard. You'll find few better examples of a company delivering impact.

5 Exposure

Hype and the Channel

Here's how to tell if your content is hype, or if it really matters. This distinction is vitally important, especially if you are trying to build a lasting audience. Are you connecting with people over the long term, or are you distracting them in an attempt to give yourself a chance? Figuring this out is key. So here's a quick checklist.

- ❏ Your material is something someone would be delighted to come across.

- ❏ You, your department, your company, or your clients look forward to what you send them.

- ❏ Your content is like a television show (not an advertisement).

These items aren't trivial. They are part of a constant self-analysis necessary to the pursuit of platform in the digital age.

Super Bowl aside, the reality is that people no longer care about advertising and don't seek it out. As we write this, immediately after the 2012 Super Bowl, we can easily recall that Matthew Broderick was in a clever ad that parodied *Ferris Bueller's Day Off.* But can we remember the car advertised? Definitely not, and it's likely that you can't either.

The attention you can get through hype is huge, and if you happen to have your own Super Bowl ad, you'll see how it works. The traffic to your Web site or project looks like a bell curve—it's huge during the commercial and shortly thereafter, but it flatlines afterward.

Let's compare this to a blog. First of all, it isn't expensive to build, which is good, because you probably don't have $3.5 million to spend anyway. Instead of money, you're being diligent, building something one day at a time. Slow, incremental improvement on your channel will also teach you a lot more than a superstar director working on your thirty-second spot.

Once you get someone interested in the work on your blog, Twitter account, etc., you've got them not just today but tomorrow as well. If you have a YouTube channel that's just starting out, and someone subscribes, you don't need to ask him or her to subscribe again. You can work on the second person in line instead, which is easier because now it's you *and* your first subscriber convincing that person. Same with the third person, who has you and two others to convince him or her, and so on. It gets easier over time, with the 101st easier than the first, and the 1,001st easier still.

If we were to look at the impact curve of a channel you own, it would not look like a bell curve—up then down, flatlining quickly—but a continuous, never-ending mountain. Over time the peaks get higher; you see the line climb to heights unimaginable. And just as each step up a mountain seems easy and eventually leads to huge heights, each step in building audience is easy, and unlike with hype, you don't immediately fall to zero afterward.

In other words, hype dies, but the channel you build is forever.

But here's the thing. Buying advertising is easy. Any kind of hype is easy. But others own the channel, so you can't control it. Besides, by definition hype is a distraction from what people are there to watch. When *Mad Men* is on, you're not waiting anxiously for Banana Republic to interrupt the show.

So besides their impact curves, the main difference between of hype and your channel is this: When you have a channel, people who watch it actually give a damn.

What Is Exposure?

Exposure is the art of hitting people, again and again, until they finally decide to take some kind of action. At its simplest, Exposure is frequency. It's what makes the prospective car buyer finally walk into the Nissan dealership or what happens when the blogger is finally able to convince readers to give him their e-mail addresses. It's what happens when the *New York Times* finally gets someone to agree that yes, perhaps its offering is worth paying premium prices for.

All of it comes down to Exposure: making sure that you are everywhere without offending the hell out of your prospective audience. It is an art, and those who manage it do it very well. Those who fail are tossed in the spam folder. Exposure has proven itself to be delicate.

At one end of the spectrum is something so innocuous we would never consider it advertising—or even a repeat, since every impression is a unique experience. At the other end is a telemarketer, who connects to us at the most inopportune moment, with the worst possible style, using what should be the most intimate medium available.

No matter what happens with your message, you will land somewhere along this spectrum. Of all the things we do, let's make sure we get this one right. It encompasses everything from the basic questions, such as how often to blog, to the more subtle ones, such as how many ways your message should be crafted.

Exposure, when done right, isn't even noticed. It's when an idea gets spread through many different means and remixed by each participant so it's slightly different. Or it's when people are exposed to your personal brand multiple times, through a variety of ideas or projects, so it seems new to them.

The following will be a practical guide to doing Exposure right. Like the rest of us, you're probably doing part of it well, but there can still be some improvement. Let's get started.

The Fallacy of Needing a Vast Platform

We've each come to a different opinion about the ideal frequency of contact in building platform. Chris spent a number of years blogging daily, sometimes more than once a day, while Julien decided that blogging weekly, sometimes every two weeks, was plenty. The numbers suggest that Chris has more readers. But does that translate into more business opportunities?

It's not an apples-to-apples situation. Julien's business comes from different sources than that of Chris, who benefits from blog posts that educate prospective buyers on what Chris might be able to do for their industries. Second, tracking leads is something neither of us does with any kind of vigor, so this information is somewhat anecdotal. But what Chris has discovered regarding the differences between our two platforms is worth considering.

Blogging frequency does impact number of subscribers, and this can be easily measured. Post once a week and your subscriber count goes down. Post once a day and your subscriber count rises. Post three times a day and it rises even more. However, volume of subscribers isn't especially useful unless you're working in a "cost per impression" (CPM) business. When Chris experimented with posting less frequently to his blog, his subscriber count went down, but the quality of comments and the general level of interaction stayed even. However, this impacted Chris's social proof. His rank in the top five of the *Advertising Age* Power 150 slipped to seven. Is this earth-shattering? No, but it means something to some people.

On social networks, multitudes of "simple touches," such as quick responses to people via Twitter, stack up in recipients' minds as a sign that you see them and respect them and like interacting with them. This translates to a great deal of positive sentiment. In this case, experimenting with fewer updates didn't matter, unless the kind of updates that suddenly declined were the positive responses to other people's posts. Commenting and replying, it turns out, are much more valuable than posting your own original content, as far as engagement and response metrics indicate. On social networks, posting less frequently reduces the rate at which new people follow you, but it doesn't often translate to a drop-off in subscribers.

Quality of contact was interesting to experiment with. Julien began weekly phone calls with people he felt he could learn from, as well as people he might be able to help, and he reported great value from these meetings. Chris refocused some of his social-media following and attention on a smaller set of people who were good connectors or had other value to him, instead of following everyone who chose to connect with him, and the impact was immediate and tangible.

It appears that a vast platform doesn't immediately mean a bigger impact, though neither of us dismisses the potential boost that arises when one is more widely known. Neither of us has been offered a perfume line like Kim Kardashian, nor do either of us have any requests to stop wearing certain products, à la Mike "The Situation" Sorrentino from *Jersey Shore*, who received a note from Abercrombie & Fitch offering to pay him to *stop* wearing its clothes.

The focus, we suspect, should be on filling your platform with a number of high-quality connectors and nurturing relationships that share value between yourself and that network. It's okay to embrace and interact with others who aren't as good at connecting or who don't offer the same level of opportunities to your future, of course. We're not advocating that you be strictly business about building your platform—that's just being a straight-up cad. We're saying that when you focus more attention on your relationships with connectors, platform size matters less.

Okay, but How Often Should I Blog?

Ever since blogging began, bloggers have asked, "How often should I blog?" It falls neatly into the category of questions like "How long is a piece of string?" You should blog as often as you have ideas to blog about. You should blog as often as you have something amazing to say.

If you're looking for numbers and statistics, they exist, but they're generic and definitely not a one-size-fits-all formula. We've experimented a lot with this, though. Here's what we know from our own experiments.

1. If you blog daily, your number of subscribers will go up (almost without fail, but with some kind of cutoff at the higher numbers if your posts are crap).

2. If you blog twice or more daily, your number of subscribers will go up even more.

3. If you blog weekly, you won't necessarily lose subscribers.

4. If you blog monthly, you might lose subscribers, or you might not.

5. Sunday is a kind of magical day for releasing a blog post, because it appears that people take a break at some point during that day to catch up on nonhome matters, and they comment just a bit longer, visit just a bit longer, and more. Why? No idea. But every time we post on Sunday, the results are pretty good.

6. There's no magical time of day to post a blog. Chris likes to post by 4:30 A.M. Eastern time, but he has some readers in India and the UK, in addition to those in the United States. It's always at a weird time somewhere in the system. That said, posting around anyone's 5:00 P.M. on a Friday isn't a good idea.

We worried about these things too, when we thought they made a difference. The truth is, they don't. When you post and how often you post don't matter nearly as much as whether you're posting information that other people can use and relate to, information that will prompt them to maintain some kind of relationship with you.

The point is, unless you're trying to be a media property, like a new magazine or breaking-news source, you don't need to post more than once or twice a week. In a world where everyone seems to malign the reality of 24-7 news coverage, why would you seek to emulate it?

Realize, though: People's consumption habits are very real, and their consumption is growing. The rise of tablets and other "lean back" devices means that people are seeking more and more passive entertainment and information and consuming it without ever really digging too deep.

Playing the "how many subscribers" game once seemed like the way to do things, but the real metric is, as it has always been, "Who takes action when I ask?" That's the metric you want to measure.

How often should you blog? As often as you can get a reaction that's useful to your pursuits. As often as you can serve your community. That's how often. Don't have time to blog? Well, no one has time for anything. That's not what you're asking us.

The "Look at Me" Problem

The "look at me" problem is a big reason why people go wrong with the Exposure part of the Impact Equation. We call it this because it's what kids spend a lot of their time saying. "Look at me, Mom!" Essentially, we are so hungry for attention that we overwhelm people with a need to be seen . . . and it backfires.

Exposure and Being Seen

There's a difference between Exposure and attention. Exposure is a blend of opportunity and the ability to be part of various platforms. Jimmy Fallon has a late-night television show that gives him a lot of Exposure. From this, he has the ability to earn attention. People without that kind of access might struggle to be seen, crave attention, and lack Exposure. The difference is profound and often misunderstood. What comes next is usually where the problem starts.

People with some level of superficial access, such as the ability to message someone via the social Web, mistake this ability for Exposure. For instance, someone might send a tweet to Ashton Kutcher to attempt to draw his attention to their issue or project. At the very moment we typed this sentence, there were approximately seventy-four people asking him for attention. Do you think he'll see any of those requests? No, not really.

So What if You're the "Unknown" Person?

Where everyone seems to get this part wrong is that they set their sights on the biggest name they can find, online or otherwise. If they think they can reach the mayor of the city, they go for that. If they have a sense that they can reach a minor celebrity, all the better. But that's not what works.

If you want success in Exposure, there are a few good strategies:

■ Start with like-minded people. If you are interested in preserving the habitat of snow owls, figure out who else is and talk to them first. You need to build some level of Exposure with those passionate about your cause before you try to raise awareness at a new level.

■ Tell stories that relate to people who don't share your cause. If you're hoping to sell people on donating bikes to people in Africa, it doesn't matter that the people in Africa know the story line. It matters that the person you're looking to get the money from understands.

■ Tell stories that make the buyer the hero. If you've built an amazing rain-gutter-screen business, who's going to care except the kind of person who is asking how to improve the value of their house?

■ Help others first. Most people fail in getting the attention of others because they approach with their hands out long before they have done anything to earn a seat at the table. If you want attention, earn it. Be helpful to others. (Hint: Retweeting someone's posts all day doesn't really count.)

Be There Ahead of Time

If you want the magic trick of all magic tricks, however, here it is: Be there before anyone even knows who you are. What do we mean? What if you're selling craft beers in Michigan? Why not be the person putting out the *Michigan Craft Brewer's Monthly* magazine online? You're suddenly the person people come to regard before they even know that you're part of the space. See?

The trick, again, is to represent other brewers equally. It wouldn't do to highlight your own products more than anyone else's. People will notice, and you'll lose credibility. In fact, disclose everything. Talk about the fact that you too are part of the ecosystem you're writing about. The more you can position yourself to be the person covering the space while being part of the space, the more chance you'll earn credibility while gaining Exposure.

Jeremiah Owyang did this a long time ago while working for Hitachi Data Systems. He created a very useful wiki site for all the various large storage companies, who were promoting competing products, along with his own products. People knew that Jeremiah represented Hitachi, but they found his site so useful that they considered his products alongside the other companies' products and sometimes bought his, simply because they appreciated all his hard work in covering the space.

It's amazing how few companies take this approach. They prefer the "What? We have no competitors. You've never even heard of them. Look over here! It's *our* product!" approach. This is silly, but you see it all the time. You see credit card companies and automobile companies that refuse to mention their competition when they should. And what comes of it? A diminished sense of Trust.

Want to get a lot more Exposure? Learn to be the go-to resource instead of begging for scraps from people you perceive to be powerful.

How to Do Exposure Wrong

The only real way to do Exposure wrong is to betray the sacred places your audience members set for themselves.

A sacred place, for the purpose of our conversation, is an implicit part of the social contract you build with your audience member. Every person in the world has one, whether it's their place of worship (literally) or their e-mail in-box.

But the irony of the sacred place is that you cannot assume what your readers consider valuable and what territory is okay to step upon. Some are comfortable with blogs in their in-box, while others find it immensely distracting and invasive, but how do you tell which is which?

The reality of Exposure is that, in order to understand it, you must sometimes break the social code you have built with your audience *purposefully*—but delicately, of course.

How to Break the Social Contract

Breaking the social contract is a difficult part of making progress with your audience, especially when you don't explicitly know what it is they do or don't want. Your understanding of your audience is limited—you may see they spend a long time on your site, for example, but not know why. You might think you know from the comments, but they may not be representative of the entire group.

Your understanding of your audience is necessarily incomplete and always will be. This was true even when one saw one's audience face-to-face, and it's even truer in the media channels we use today.

The only way to truly understand how your audience members

feel is to see what happens when you try new things. You only discover the limits of Exposure when you hit your audience too often or in an offensive or different way so that they change their behavior (causing changes in your analytics—bounce rate, time on site, or what have you), react via comments, or begin to leave altogether.

So if you have any anxiety about any of these things, it's best to get rid of it now. Perhaps take a look at Julien's book *The Flinch*, or his blog (inoveryourhead.net), where you will see how offensive content can be and still work. Once you overcome the fear of losing your audience, you will discover that experimentation's apparent risk usually leads to high reward.

Mapping Out Your Audience's Values

Every piece of content your channel creates should be considered an experiment. What do your readers send out to others? How do they gel with the stuff you've made? The more content you create, the better you will know, and even the failures will teach you about what matters to them. As your content gets spread out and hits different parts of the Web, the creation of an ideal reader or audience is perhaps one of the most valuable processes available.

Our friend James Chartrand first guided us to this idea, and you can find out more about it on MenWithPens.ca. Here's something Julien wrote for his blog a long time ago, when he was first trying to figure out who his readers should be. The process he used to create it is called freewriting; he wrote down everything that came into his head without judgment in order to have the longest possible list. Try it. After all ideas are down on paper, use this exercise to create a list of descriptors for your prospective audience, such as "cynical," "friendly," or "just starting out."

IDEAL READER EXERCISE FOR JULIEN'S BLOG

The ideal reader is a person in his or her twenties or thirties.

He reads this blog first thing in the morning.

He either works for himself or has some job where he is not totally happy—maybe advertising or online marketing, but something related to an interest of Julien's. Or he might have a normal but boring job, like Julien once did.

He is eco-conscious. He is liberal (or maybe libertarian). He is "socially liberal but fiscally conservative."

He is urban, or at least has an urban mind-set. He is from New York instead of, say, Omaha. He is kind of cynical.

He might be married, but he is "free." He wants more out of life and has the ability to get it but just can't seem to take the necessary steps.

He might have kids. He might have pets. He probably has neither.

He is college educated but is not working in the industry he was educated in. Continuing his education/learning is important to him.

He is an overachiever—or he wants to be.

He is otherwise an ordinary dude, whatever that means. Like everyone else, he has some quirky traits, but he's not crazy out there or something. Julien is much weirder than he is. That, maybe, is why he is interested in Julien's blog.

The ideal reader, like Julien, has an activist mind-set.

Whatever the case, he wants everything out of life—as Julien does. Whatever part of him that ideal life appeals to, that is the part Julien speaks to.

You can see now that only after imagining an ideal reader (and experimenting against it) can we see what kind of people are paying attention to a certain channel and what their values are. You can also get a sense by watching their responses. Fox News viewers, for example, may become upset at a poll stating that President Obama's attempts to reduce unemployment are working, while BBC viewers may become upset if something interrupts *Coronation Street*. In other words, their values become evident based on what they feel is worth talking about.

The Coming Oversaturation Issue

We've talked a lot about online channels and the great opportunities that come with them, but there is one major pending problem. Those of us using these new tools to connect and communicate are now facing saturation. See if this resonates with you.

You get about two hundred or more e-mails a day. You have a few hundred friends and connections on Facebook, some of whom post updates quite often. You have a Twitter account where all the other people you follow post even more updates. You read a bunch of blogs and online news sources. You watch videos on YouTube, TED.com, and Hulu.

Be honest. There's so much going on that you're even losing track of the people who matter most to you. You're skipping half of the newsletters you subscribe to. You're not keeping up with e-mail. And yet at the same time you feel this hunger to consume information and learn more, for fear of being left behind or in hopes of finding that next big thing.

You're not alone. Everyone we know is experiencing the same set of issues, and that includes your target audience. What can you do about it? How do you rise above the noise? Here's a tool kit.

Purposeful Media Making

First, realize that every post you make to a social channel (including e-mail) is information. You are adding information to the queue for people who have opted in to receiving that information. People judge the value of what you share.

Depending on how you want to use your platform, you must consider how to make your information purposeful. You don't have to be strictly serious. Please don't let us get you thinking that you need to button up tightly and not share your personable side. That wouldn't do at all. We both advocate being very human.

But we do want you to be purposeful. Ask yourself whom you're trying to attract with the information you're sharing. Then ask yourself whether what you're sharing will be useful, interesting, entertaining, or compelling to that person. Remember what we said in part 1 about being a fledgling TV station? That applies here.

Brevity and Mobile Rules

The rising trend cannot be avoided: Smart phones and tablet computers are outpacing laptops and desktops as the information-consumption product of choice. More and more people are connecting to everything you share with a three-inch screen or a seven-inch screen. If you're not creating your information so that it plays well on a mobile device, you're going to lose ground in the platform game. If you're not brief enough to be consumed by someone thumbing through a smart phone, you'll lose them.

Here are some quick fixes to implement now (not next month).

■ Configure a mobile version of your Web site (or sites). This doesn't cost much. The real effort is in understanding what someone *most* wants to do with your Web site while not at their desk. The answer isn't always the same as the experience you offer on a larger screen.

■ Throw out the fancy HTML e-mail newsletter templates and go thinner. You can still use HTML, but use more text and less graphics.

■ Simplify e-mails to a single call to action, and lead with a sentence that explains the most important point you're trying to make. People read the first line or two of your e-mail and decide whether or not to reply. You have about twenty-five words to hook someone into taking action. Choose wisely.

Consumption Nation

People are chewing through content faster than ever. That's the almost-good news. The bad news is that they want it simpler and simpler. People aren't reading *Moby-Dick* anymore. They are reading bite-size posts and moving into visual formats like video and informational graphics. If you want to keep your platform alive, you have to create for their tastes.

Consider e-books, video, and infographics. People are consuming more than ever before, but they're less interested in simple text. Create e-books for their tablets and readers. Create video for them to consume in small bites (three minutes or less). Make infographics or draw pictures that explain complex ideas or numbers in simple visual formats.

Again, brevity rules. Everything you're making should be modular, easy to download to a mobile device, and compelling enough to keep someone's attention.

The Dangers of Cross-Wiring Your Social Channels

The oversaturation problem is exacerbated when you choose to post the same information across several channels, perhaps with a push-to-many service. Plus, the current trend for many social platforms is to cross-populate on your behalf. For instance, many people have wired their Foursquare (location-based check-in service) updates to populate on Twitter and elsewhere. Many people have linked their Twitter account to their LinkedIn account. There are issues with all of this.

If you cross-post the same content to all of your social channels, people who subscribe to you in more than one channel will receive it more than once, making it far less likely to compel them to take action. Further, some of these people will decide to unfollow or unsubscribe from you on whichever channel they value the most and relegate you to a back burner, hurting your ability to grow and maintain a healthy platform.

Instead, consider creating a unique spin on the content for each platform. A tweet is very different from a Facebook or Google+ update, and you would phrase a lead-in to your information on LinkedIn differently from content on any of those platforms. See how that works?

By overlapping, you're throwing information into a platform that might not benefit from having it. Look at your last twenty tweets. Would you want them all showing up on LinkedIn? We bet not. If you're checking in on Foursquare and your client sees five Starbucks trips over the course of the day while you're behind on your deadline, how beneficial will that be?

Sever the connections. It all works better when you treat each network like its own beast.

So what *should* you do?

Oversaturation Is Real

This issue is already afoot. The name of the game is to penetrate the noise and clutter and to build impact and value.

Contrast is a matter of standing out from the oversaturation. Exposure is an issue. You must find ways to connect with people and capture their attention, but if you stuff the box, so to speak, you'll find yourself ignored. Echo is important, as you'll want to share information that resonates with those people you're trying to build relationships with. This merits a lot of consideration.

How Not to Wear Out Your Welcome: High Exposure Done Right

If you're working to get more and more Exposure and improve your potential for impact, there are ways to do that where you'll grow and ways that will cause everyone to sneer at best and revolt at worst. The line between Exposure being good for you and Exposure turning people against you is hair thin, and we can't articulate it very well for you. Perhaps, though, we can offer insight into what helps and what hurts people's perspectives.

The iPod shipped with sleek white earbuds (not even earphones) because from a gazillion miles away, they indicated that you were using an iPod. The more we saw those earbuds around, the more we thought about the iPod. This got us thinking more about buying one, and then, suddenly, we too were sporting those earbuds and signaling to others that they might consider buying an iPod too.

What's interesting is that Exposure is one of the core elements of being a powerful disruptor. Most people tend to believe that when there's an ingrained leader in a certain space there's no sense in challenging them. What we've come to realize, however, is that there are always new ways of slicing a marketplace and for enterprising and risk-taking types to lead.

Kevin Plank did. He was facing a big fork in the road at the end of his college career. He was doing okay at football but knew he probably couldn't go all the way with it. He had a big job offer from Prudential Life Insurance, but he felt like that would suck his life away.

But he also had an idea. He created a performance fabric and made shirts from it, which in and of itself wouldn't have given him much hope of success. What did was that he realized he wasn't going to sell it strictly to athletes. The mainstream would consider buying the shirts if he could get enough Exposure and professional endorsement.

In a relatively brief amount of time, Under Armour has grown to half the size of Nike (its biggest competitor) and has dwarfed much of the competition. Its logo is becoming as recognizable as the world-famous swoosh. This disruptive brand came to be because Kevin Plank networked and got his shirt onto the backs of as many professional athletes as he could. He leveraged that Exposure to get more professional deals, while he was well positioned to sell directly to the consumers who wanted to wear what their champions wore.

Under Armour won almost strictly through Exposure, beyond the other Impact Attributes.

There are many ways to think about getting Exposure. You can get product placement within larger media channels. You can push for reviews. You can look for celebrity endorsements. You can do giveaways at certain events that will get people thinking about giving something new a try.

When we think about Exposure of ideas or of people, that's where it starts to get more complicated.

Live from New York

Saturday Night Live has a kind of magic to it. It may be amazing, or it may be simply okay. It may blow your mind, or it may simply blow, but whatever happens, if you're at home on a Saturday night, don't you worry. *SNL* will be there.

Exposure, when done right, is a magical thing. It creates a default status in the mind of the recipient, saying to him or her, "Well, if there's nothing else to do, there's always this." For Saturday night, it's *Saturday Night Live*—and hey, the day it plays on television is hard to forget when it's in the name. But you can take advantage of this anytime you like.

The grooves that form in the brain due to recurring activity are deep. If you brush your teeth every day upon awakening—or even better, if you chain it to another activity, such as showering—the act becomes automatic. It becomes almost impossible not to do. The same thing works with media. There may be an infinite number of channels, but the reality is that you just have to be among the top ten sites your audience thinks of at any given moment. Julien's favorite blogs—SethGodin.Typepad.com, AVC.com, and Kottke.org—are what he defaults to when there's nothing else to do. It's human nature to develop patterns, so all you have to do is increase Exposure (and keep the quality high) to place yourself inside them. This is the same reason you probably remember your childhood phone number.

When Chris and Julien first met during the early days of podcasting, one of everyone's favorite podcasts was the Daily Source Code. Hosted by former MTV VJ Adam Curry, it ran every single day, with few exceptions, and became the default for a huge number of podcast listeners, especially those with an hour-long commute. They were ready with their hour of driving, and Curry was ready with his podcast; it was an unbroken social contract that lasted almost five years.

The show wasn't always magic, of course—perfectionists need not apply here—but nobody expects media to be perfect. Instead, it works more like a glass that suddenly overflows with water when the last drop falls into it. Either it was good or it wasn't. The Web site Rotten Tomatoes works similarly: At 59 percent, a movie is "rotten"; at 60 percent, it suddenly becomes "fresh."

As long as you can stifle your perfectionism, increasing Exposure this way actually has a kind of power. The producers of *Saturday Night Live* could wait until the show was perfect every time if they wanted, but they don't; they go for it, with whatever material they have, on Saturday night. It creates some groan moments, yes, but it also creates magic on occasion by increasing the pressure on the creators. More environmental pressure means more evolution. Same goes for you.

Okay, but How Often Should I Tweet?

First off, please just feel as stupid as you should for having to use words like "tweet" and trying to look serious while saying them. We do. Tweet, blog, wiki, Pinterest, and the whole steaming lot of these words are just utterly useless and make us feel like we're in a nursery. But it's okay. You're among friends. We can say "tweet" and realize that what we're really saying is "communicate with people on these social networks."

Everyone has an opinion on this, and some companies even spend a great deal of time creating metrics and measurements and charts to determine the most powerful and appropriate way to tweet. There are hundreds (thousands? . . . sigh) of posts by bloggers and social-media experts telling you that you're doing it wrong and they know how to do it better.

As with everything else, the metrics offer some guidelines, and there are always ways to do things worse or better. We'll share with you what we know.

1. Chris's Twitter stream is stuffed full of replies to other people, which is supposed to be a no-no, because replying isn't very good information. Every time Chris replies, he gains a few hundred more followers, because people feel seen (a basic human need/desire).

2. Tweeting on-topic information all the time is a surefire way to get nowhere. It makes you a robotic news stream and not someone of interest worth paying attention to. Learning how to be interestingly off topic while still serving those who choose to follow you is a wonderful goal.

3. Tweeting over a hundred times a day will likely relegate you to some less viewed list or get you unfollowed. And yet there's someone for everyone. We follow @guykawasaki's Twitter account, knowing full well that it is supernoisy, is ghostwritten by several people, is full of programmed messages, and doesn't really have much to do with Guy Kawasaki the person anymore. Why? Because we like what he has to say. (And he's a friend.)

4. Tweeting four times a day, every six hours, would at least mean that you've covered all the time zones in some form or fashion.

5. We both advocate replying to people and being conversational in our Twitter streams. Others choose to use it like a news feed, and that's okay (probably even successful). We just do it differently, and it seems to work well for us.

There are many other ways you can "do it wrong" with Twitter. You can use programmed tweets (we do). You can choose to have a logo instead of a picture of your head (we don't). You can tweet out sales and offers instead of whatever else you're supposed to say (we do). You can talk off topic (we do). Believe us, if there's a way for someone to say you're doing it wrong, they will. There are a few ways that you can use Twitter that aren't ideal, but for the most part, you'll experiment and learn those for yourself. You don't need us for that.

#

If we've learned anything from the mass-media age, it's that if we are bombarded with a jingle for long enough, it will eventually get stuck in our heads, and perhaps we'll eventually want to buy it, whatever it is. Exposure is perhaps the most familiar Impact Attribute, the one that the general public will understand intuitively. But there are many ways to get Exposure wrong, as we've said, so it's really about how to get it right.

At one end of the Exposure spectrum is personal conversation. It isn't scalable. It happens once, with only one person as the recipient. It's in person, so it's deeply influential. Exposure is low, but other Impact Attributes (Trust, etc.) are high, so it doesn't matter. It's a sales pitch or a personal favor. It works because of the relationship, not because it's repeated.

On the other end is spam. E-mail is one of the most scalable things of all. It costs nothing to send to millions, even billions of people. It can be hitting you over and over again, perhaps thousands of times a day. Exposure is massively high, but impact is supremely low. Spam is a testament to needing multiple Impact Attributes in order to successfully spread a message.

But between these two extremes are things that work. Even some spam works with people who aren't sensitive to deception. Assuming your audience is a little skeptical, you'll want to work on Trust, Echo, and other attributes, and if both Trust and Echo work well, and you maintain variety, you can keep Exposure high too.

Interestingly enough, as we were writing this section, a donation-request e-mail came in from Wikipedia. Since it is a perfect example of a high-Exposure, high-impact, and high-Trust message, let's talk about it. After all, it worked on us (we just donated twenty dollars, and hey, maybe you should too).

Wikipedia is high Trust because you've connected with the Web site, and perhaps seen the face of its founder, Jimmy Wales, multiple times in a nonsales environment. You think of Wikipedia every day, or at least every week, as you search for anything under the sun and it tells you about it, for free. Most of the time when you connect to Wikipedia it doesn't try to get you to do anything. But around once a year, Wikipedia turns the Exposure knob way up during a donation drive, asking you and every other user to donate to the site until it reaches its goal. (It does this to make sure it stays advertising and influence free.)

Another way to look at this is that all year, Wikipedia's Exposure rating is ideally high. It never connects to you, but you're always connecting to it to find out all the stuff you're curious about. So Trust remains high, building and building all year, until the pledge drive. Some people become slightly annoyed (we aren't), but since it doesn't last long, Trust begins to rebuild immediately after.

To us, this is a perfect use of Exposure. We hope you liked it and it helps you understand how often to communicate and when to do it.

EXPOSURE: HOW TO RATE YOURSELF

It's up to you to experiment with how you're going to build your platform. There's not a lot you can do that will permanently damage or damn you. Experiment. See what works. You'll find the formula that works best for you.

And never presume that you'll hit some number and then be done. Platform is an active experience, a verb, like the word "love." It's like setting the thermostat in your house at seventy degrees and realizing that some days that means turning on the heat and other days it means cooling things down.

Realize that it's about keeping your contacts alive and building and maintaining relationships. Your role as the ringleader of a large experience never ends, and the Impact Equation way of looking at things means you never take your foot off the brake and instead look for ways to get even more cars into the race. It's a challenge.

Celebrate the brilliant minds that follow your platform and always recognize them as individuals loosely joined around similar ideas— never as *your* community and least of all as "you guys." You'll have a shot at success and you'll have a chance to improve on your own impact by nurturing relationships that matter to your larger story.

We have a whole section about the human element, and this is where people seem to fall down the most. If you thought figuring out a platform was difficult, you'll realize in no time that the hardest work is what used to be (somewhat snidely) called the "soft skills" and that very few successful ventures exist without understanding the human aspects of impact.

That's where we're going next.

IMPACT EXAMPLE: RACHEL HAWKINS

Rachel Hawkins is an author, most recently of a series of young-adult books about Sophie Mercer, a young girl sent to Hecate Hall (better known as "Hex Hall"), a kind of boarding school for not-so-quiet witches, shape-shifters, and fairies, who are normally supposed to be quiet and blend into the crowd. The books are targeted to young-adult readers, the kind who love *Twilight*, *The Hunger Games*, and the like.

Chris picked up Rachel's first book on Kindle based on a recommendation and read through it quickly. He's not exactly the target reader for the series, but it was a fun, fast read, and he enjoyed it. One quick Google search later, he'd found Rachel Hawkins on Twitter (@ladyhawkins). He sent her a quick message:

"@ladyhawkins: just finished Hex Hall! Tons of fun, though I'm not at all your demographic."

Within two minutes, Hawkins wrote back:

"@chrisbrogan: Ah, thank you so much! and I always appreciate my Grown Dude Readers:)"

Does this kind of interaction generate impact? We say yes. But let's look at the attributes of the equation.

Contrast: Rachel's book doesn't exactly stand out from others in its genre. Young adult/teen fiction, and more specifically paranormal teen romance fiction, is having a renaissance the likes of which has never been seen on American soil. *But* having a conversation with an author via Twitter most certainly sets Rachel apart from other authors. (Chris also gushed all over young-adult author Scott Westerfeld, who wasn't as responsive.[2]

Reach: Rachel has the same Reach as most authors. She put out a book that has to fight with other books on the shelf. Does she have

---

2   See http://www.chrisbrogan.com/the-opportunities-authors-might-miss/.

anything special here? No. But Rachel is quite active on Twitter, Tumblr, Facebook, and beyond and does a great job of building community among her readers and fans. Again, this gives her more Reach than some authors, who might have sold better in the past but who have yet to perceive the "threat" of Rachel Hawkins earning her place among her fans.

Exposure: Here we can kind of "ditto" the above points. Rachel has low Exposure the way most fiction authors do: She releases books very seldom. But her use of social platforms to build community gets her out there a little more. Watching her blog is amazing. She connects with readers regularly and on many subjects, not just the books themselves, and every post her readers receive teaches her audience a little bit more about her, which helps sell the books when they're released.

Articulation: Rachel's series, Hex Hall, does a great job of walking that perfect line of being parent-approved while seeming naughty enough. But what also works for Rachel is that she defines the guts of the books quite well. They're about feeling that you don't fit in, that everyone's hiding something from you, that there's more to everything than what you see.

Trust: Rachel has been around a while. Her Trust is solid with her audience, and although Chris isn't in her target demographic, her quick response to him shows reliability, an aspect of Trust.

Echo: Rachel *is* her community. She gushes about *Game of Thrones* on her Tumblr.[3] She writes funny tweets about fantasy books. She's exactly like the people who read her writing. Notice that I'm not talking about her character, Sophie Mercer, or any of the other well-crafted people roaming her series. I'm talking about Rachel. She's got a great Impact Equation because when people get to know the person

---

3   See http://hexybellerachel.tumblr.com/.

behind the books, they realize they've just met themselves, and now they *really* want her to succeed. That's golden.

There's a key lesson here: Your product or service might not stand out on its own. If you sell insurance, for example, your policies are likely similar to everyone else's, but if you can do something to make you, yourself, more interesting and engaging and embody the attributes of the Impact Equation, you have a chance.

There are a few big-name fiction authors who do a great job communicating with their fans and turning them into online communities. In Rachel's genre, our favorite is Neil Gaiman, who started blogging back in the nineties, around when Chris started, and was at the same event where we did our first-ever book signing of *Trust Agents*. Neil actively makes his community feel seen and heard. But he's also a powerhouse in his field and probably doesn't need to work the Impact Equation to succeed.

Rachel Hawkins, however, earns her way over many other aspiring and published-but-not-very-seen authors by the very way she puts herself out there. You might look at this example and say, "So what? Anyone can do that." Here's the hint: Anyone *can* do that. Rachel is getting buyers because she *does* do it.

PART **4** Network

Congratulations, you have reached the final part of the roller coaster. You have screamed, and your heart is pumping in your chest. You may even be ready to stop, but we're not done yet. The most important Impact Attributes are yet to come.

You may have a wide Reach, a massive platform that enables you to connect with everyone. Your idea may be genius, and it may be caught immediately imprinted onto people's brains. You may be differentiated from your industry and highly visible. But if you are not trusted, if you are not credible, you are nothing.

Though Trust was the subject of our last book, we didn't delve into the real details of how it works, how people come to believe in one another, and how networks grow. We never discussed the secret sauce of getting into someone's inner circle, partly due to space constraints but also because the obsession with social networks (the new thing!) at the time was so high that we obsessed about the tool instead of the human.

Today we are here to correct that. As we have said before, if you come away from this book unable to foresee success in the impact of your venture, if you leave unable to make a better impression on people than when you began, we have failed.

We want to explain the human element in such a way that it becomes indelible in your mind. What you're doing right, or wrong, must be immediately clear to you, as if a coach were watching over your shoulder throughout your interactions.

For us, this is also the most daunting part of the book. Why? It is the softest, the most unquantifiable of all of the elements of our equation. Thankfully, it is also the place where we stand in the shadows of giants.

What makes people trust one another is a subject that has fascinated people since the beginning of time—and it shows. From *How to Win Friends and Influence People* to *The Trusted Advisor*, this subject has been at the core of business for a long time. It has never vanished because human relationships, in reality, are never truly mastered.

The reality is that the study of Trust, credibility, and all of the soft skills is never truly done. There's always more to learn—always another aspect that eludes us, maybe forever. Yet, there are some things that are set in stone, sets of best practices that most people know yet do not perform. One of our goals is to get you up to speed.

Methods for community building have always existed, yet the best methods for developing community have never truly been deciphered, especially with the new complexities of online interaction. We often see supposed experts making the same mistakes as beginners, proving once again that the lessons are never truly done.

You have to see yourself as a constant student if you are interested in making progress in any human art form, whether it's salesmanship, network building, or anything else. Improvement is always possible, and we hope to teach you a thing or two.

Audience, Community, and Network

Quite often people will say they have a community built around their business, or they have a huge community following them on such and such a social network. We would disagree. More often people have an audience, and that audience is essentially some number of people who have opted in to receiving information from them. An audience can be a physical one, like people at a conference, or it can be a group of people who receive a newsletter. But never mistake an audience for a community.

Your community are those people who work to maintain an ongoing interaction with you. And never, ever make the mistake of crowning yourself the king or queen of that community. Instead, realize that you have the privilege and honor to serve the community, even if they have chosen to gather around your ideas, your products or services, or something else of your creation. And always realize that communities in this context are loosely joined and quick to disperse.

Say you're an Apple fan and you love your MacBook Air, for instance. You might even participate in MacBook- or Apple-related forums online. You might supply ideas, advice, or helpful information to other Mac users. We know quite a few people who self-identify as Apple fans, but very few of them consider that a primary identity label. You might be a huge Nine Inch Nails fan, but unless you're running the Santa Barbara chapter of the club, you probably consider that just one part of your identity.

You belong to several communities. You own a Camaro and keep up with news and shared information in that space. You practice Krav Maga and keep up to speed with the big names in that space. You listen to Bob Marley and know the tribute bands. You also watch *Adventure Time* and love Finn the Human enough to wear T-shirts featuring him. Usually we don't align with just one community. And yet nurturing those who choose to spend some of their time, attention, and effort contributing to the community you're fortunate enough to serve should be a priority.

A network is something different. A network spans more than one community. If we need someone with mobile-marketing skills or experience-marketing knowledge, we know to bother Tim Hayden in Austin, Texas. If we want someone in the technical side of the digital-publishing industry, we bother Hugh McGuire from PressBooks in Canada. We know that Joel Libava is experienced with franchises. We have learned how to nurture networks that span many different countries and many different needs.

Three Very Different Interactions

The way you spend your time with these three types of people depends on how each contributes to your own success and value. If you run a transactional business, like selling more burgers for some marginal amount of profit, then an audience will suit that need just fine. You don't need to nurture a burger community. You probably don't even need a network to help you get this job done. If you're selling a high-priced product that has a very long sales lead cycle, a community would be a great investment of your time and effort, because the referrals that come from such a community would help you immensely. If you work in multiple verticals or niches, a varied network is vital to your survival.

We would argue that having a decent network is important no matter what business you find yourself in. Further, we feel that many people don't do enough to nurture and diversify their network, and they usually find this out after they lose their job. Time and time again we receive e-mails from people who find themselves suddenly out of work, and time and time again we find ourselves asked to help get them back on track. We usually haven't heard from these people for a year at least, and then their first interaction with us is a request for help in finding work. See why that doesn't usually work well?

Maintaining a community takes a lot of time and effort, and it's the hardest return-on-investment sell in the world to convince your employer (or sometimes yourself) of its direct and instant worth. And yet book after book presents case studies showing the benefit of having a strong community.

Industries That Would Benefit from a Community-Nurturing Approach

The human elements of the Impact Equation work really well for businesses that require more than a simple transaction to complete a sale.

- Real estate works much better with a community element. Become the hub of neighborhood news and business matchmaking, and you will find yourself getting calls often.

- Business-to-business products and services are great for community-based sales, because you can link noncompeting customers together to talk about successful recipes for using your products, which encourages more use and sales.

- Complex products like software and creative products like cameras or musical instruments benefit from having communities, because what you make with them (like photos, music, or Word documents) becomes public. Further, a community permits people to cross-educate and solve minor issues without the company's intervention. Dell, for example, has very active user-driven forums where people often solve one another's problems without any Dell-badged employee intervening.

■ Communities of like-minded individuals often form. For instance, if you're the type of person who loves *Entrepreneur* magazine, you probably want to speak with other readers. These communities can form easily if there is often new material for them to interact with. For instance, beer lovers can talk about new brews they've experienced. Look at Yelp. Some people go there to read reviews, but others consider themselves active Yelpers. A Yelper believes that he or she is helping others make better purchasing decisions. See the value in that?

The Value of Communities and Networks to Companies

Businesses have yet to take this to heart, with some exceptions. Some realize that the value of a salesperson is in whether he or she can build a network and get doors opened. But what does a business typically do? It builds in all kinds of restrictions on how a salesperson can and cannot interact with those connections, for fear that the salesperson will leave and take those connections with him or her.

It starts with fear. "If Sharon spends our time and money networking, and then she quits and takes those people with her, we've invested in an asset that we weren't able to utilize. Therefore, we will write rules and restrictions to make sure this doesn't happen." Thus companies confirm that a network is actually important, but then, for some reason, they forget this completely.

Should a customer-service employee be encouraged to network? Why not? Should your finance team be encouraged to network? What would be the benefit to your business's community if you added even more of your team to the experience?

Chris Grams from Red Hat (which is Linux software) told us that one of the company lawyers became quite active in the Red

Hat community. When it came time to iterate on a new version of the fedora logo, her contribution was to help people understand the legal perspective on what they were doing. Instead of being a pesky outsider, this lawyer was dead center in the experience.

We believe that everyone in the company could be adding much more value if they were permitted (and even encouraged) to build more relationships and to nurture the company's community.

How does this add value? Imagine that your prospective buyer actually knows how to reach more than just the salesperson, and that the buyer can ask a product question to the person who creates or maintains the product. How much will that aid in the buying decision? Think about how it would feel to be a paying customer of a service or product and be able to talk whenever you choose with people who provide that experience to you. (We both have this opportunity all the time, speaking with people from companies that represent products and services we use. It's a powerful and wonderfully synergistic feeling.)

This works from an acquisition standpoint: I can talk with these people, so I know more about what I intend to buy. It also works from a retention standpoint: I wasn't sure how to use this product to the best of my ability, but I'm able to talk with people to improve my usage (which, in turn, drives more adoption and future purchases). If your effort to build and maintain a platform that reaches people through the human element could drive more people to buy and more people to stay, wouldn't that be a valuable enough proposition?

We see it that way. And in these coming sections, we intend to prove it.

6 Trust

Okay, what is Trust, really? Is it a feeling, or does it have rational backing? Can it be built quickly, or does it require a bunch of time? The answer, as usual, is that it depends.

In our years at conferences, in business meetings, and in personal interactions, we've seen audiences beguiled enough in forty-five minutes that they're willing to hand a speaker a significant amount of their hard-earned money. We've also seen people screw up quickly enough to ruin years' worth of Trust in one sentence. Both are possible not because of the information the presenter gives out, but because of how he makes his audience *feel*.

In some ways, Trust is easy to understand. We all get it, and we can easily tell if we trust someone or not. Trust is about confidence and reliability. Trust is about feeling close to someone. It's easy to understand if we trust someone else, but how can we tell if someone trusts *us*? That isn't as easy.

We send thousands of subconscious signals, hundreds of times a day, to individuals we interact with. When people read our material, when they interact with us directly, and when they see us in videos or in real life, in each instance they are making basic Trust decisions, such as whether they should ask us to watch their laptop at the local café. The reason we are so good at deciding these things is because it is built into our genes, and any deviation from the norm could, at one point, have been a fatal decision.

Yet the Web is a different environment that, in some ways, changes the rules. Lots of the signals we would normally receive from others are blocked off. We now interact more through media such as Twitter and text messages than we do in real life, making our signals go haywire. Whom do we trust, and how does it happen? It's gotten a lot more complex. Fundamentally, it's the same as it has always been, but the way we send the signals transforms the entire exchange.

You may know our previous book, *Trust Agents*, in which we discussed the emergence of a new type of individual adept at using the new tools of the Web to take advantage of this transformation. If so, you'll be pleased to know that we'll go deeper into that discussion here and deal more with the really important stuff. *Trust Agents* clocked in at around three hundred pages, but here we have only around thirty, so we plan to use them wisely.

The Trust Equation

Before this book existed or was even a twinkle in our eyes, the book we were best known for was *Trust Agents*. You may have read it—a lot of people did—and if that's the case, you may have noticed that although we based it on the idea of Trust, we didn't talk much about the mechanics of how Trust works. Instead, we focused on how to build audience and be human on the Web in a general sense and assumed that an understanding of Trust would follow. Looking back on it now, however, we're not sure if this was the way it should have been done.

We often note that the best parts of books, or the best books in general, include sections that talk about things in a very detailed, clear way. The most highlighted parts of Chris's Kindle books are often the most precise ones. People seem fascinated by how many hours are spent on social media by professionals, for example, and by how many times they post and share per day. We wouldn't have guessed it, but it turns out that sometimes precision is exactly what people want.

When we wrote this book, we considered the ten-thousand-foot view, but we also knew that each Impact Attribute would need to be discussed in a concrete manner, because it's how you get ideas to stick most effectively. With that in mind, we present to you the Trust Equation, on which the whole idea of this book was constructed. For this we are much indebted to *The Trusted Advisor*, by David Maister, Charles Green, and Robert Galford.

$$C * R * I / S = TRUST$$
$$C = Credibility$$
$$R = Reliability$$
$$I = Intimacy$$
$$S = Self\text{-}interest$$

Credibility is what you say that can actually be backed up by your credentials. A *Harvard Business Review* guy is more qualified than your average Joe to talk about how Trust works in business, for example. We are (some say) more qualified to talk about building an audience on the Web than some random blogger. And so on. When credibility is high, it's often because you have qualification signals such as degrees or industry accolades.

Reliability is what happens when you do what you say you will do. For example, if you say, "I can deliver a thousand new visitors to your Web site by next week," and you do so, you are reliable. We've called reliability the Web's secret sauce because people on the Web tend to do things whenever they like, which displays low reliability So those who deliver regularly are those who win. High reliability means you do what you say you will do, often. If that doesn't seem rare to you, you clearly have never worked on the Internet.

Intimacy is a secret sauce of a different type. It ranges from "I like him, so I'll help him out" to "She really understands me" or even just "He listens." Intimacy is all levels of closeness between individuals, often for personal reasons that aren't related to business but that influence business decisions every day. Have you ever decided to work with someone just because you felt he was a good guy and deserved your business, even if he was kind of unreliable and had no credentials? Well, that's intimacy at work.

As it turns out, further studies after *The Trusted Advisor* was published proved intimacy is by far the most important part of the equation. (This is why we have given it its own name, Echo, and its own section.)

Self-interest is the final part of this equation. Just as Contrast (in our Impact Equation) is a force multiplier for everything else, self-orientation is the big problem in any trust-related transaction. If someone seems like a used-car salesman, they have a high self-orientation. If they seem like they genuinely want to help and want the best for you whether they get your business or not, they have a low self-orientation.

Self-orientation is also about knowing how to listen. Are you waiting your turn to talk, for example, or truly listening with the intent of absorbing what matters to your conversation partner? The difference between a high and low self-orientation is often subtle, because it requires an understanding of body language and other nuances that don't give themselves away easily.

In the next few segments, we're going to bring this together alongside ideas of our own that will help you understand how important Trust is to leaving a good, lasting impression on people. It isn't possible to use Trust alone to get all your goals achieved, of course; you do need people to actually hear about you and your ideas, for example. But once they're on the inside, high Trust allows your ideas to massively spread, increasing Exposure and other factors at a fraction of the time and resource cost.

Then, and Now

In writing this book, we found ourselves approaching the Trust section with the most trepidation. Many companies and individuals we researched as examples scored lowest in the Trust attribute. We want to stress that this doesn't mean we feel anyone is not trustworthy or not to be trusted. It was just harder to talk through the mechanics of Trust and harder to show a company's or individual's demonstration of it as part of impact.

And yet, over and over again, we felt that Trust was one of the most important attributes of the entire equation. A lot of the other attributes will be for naught if companies and individuals can't earn Trust and demonstrate their trustworthiness to sustain the business relationship.

When this book talked about how DollarShaveClub.com made a powerful leap from a very simple idea into something quite successful, the concern was that Trust wasn't immediately obvious and that perhaps it would take a while for the company to earn a reputation of Trust. If people felt the product was of value, was received on time, and all their transactions with the company went well, then some "noise" of that experience and reputation would filter out, and people would share indications of that Trust.

In a longish way, we're saying that Trust is one of the most elusive and difficult of the Impact Attributes, and you will have to work to earn it. It matters a great deal to your customers, your prospects, your partners, and everyone else. Small-town Trust used to be a matter of time. The same has become true of doing business on the Web, and small-town values certainly are a great way to look at Trust building for your own organization. (Grab *Small Town Rules*, by Barry Moltz and Becky McCray, as it covers that in spades.)

You might find some success without working on Trust, but we've baked the need for it into the Impact Equation for a reason. To *sustain* a strong business experience in today's marketplace, Trust will be a longer and more visible path than ever before. In a world of reviews, online complaints, and the inability to hide any bad experiences from future buyers, you'll find Trust a powerful and important attribute.

Basic Human Behaviors

During the 2010 FIFA World Cup in South Africa, the most famous participant was not an announcer, nor a soccer player, nor even a referee. It was a traditional South African instrument: the vuvuzela.

Just as you remember where you were during the *Challenger* disaster or when you heard that Princess Di had passed away, you remember the first time you heard that sound. It is horrible, and you will never forget it. You could hear it blasting throughout the audio track of every single World Cup game, deafeningly and without end. Many found the only solution was to turn the sound off entirely. Television networks applied filters to the audio of soccer games so the sound wouldn't be so disruptive.

But someone at YouTube clearly did not agree. Around the end of June 2010, YouTube introduced the vuvuzela button. Blogs, Twitter, and pretty much every other social network were flooded with expressions of shock at its appearance on every single YouTube video—that is to say, billions of them.

How did it work? Well, the vuvuzela button did one thing and one thing only: It played the vuvuzela, loudly. No matter the video, be it Bach piano concertos, Norwegian heavy metal, or Rick Astley, the vuvuzela was played at equal volume. The volume could not be turned down—it could only be turned on or off via a simple button in the shape of a soccer ball.

Take a moment to imagine the horror of this situation on a grand scale. At any given time, around the globe, hundreds of thousands, if not millions, of YouTube videos are being watched about any given subject. The vuvuzela is not a welcome addition to *any* of these videos, not even the ones about the World Cup. The vuvuzela was considered one of the most annoying cultural imports of South Africa precisely because it invaded every game a soccer fan could watch. The world did not need more vuvuzela. It needed less.

Yet here was YouTube. It had not merely talked about this internally but actually done it. Millions of vuvuzelas, all across the world, were going to be played through everyone's speakers, in offices and homes everywhere, startling some and upsetting many. Google Analytics fans could unquestionably say that this would increase bounce rate, reduce time on-site, and decrease ad clicks. In other words, it was a straight-up bad business decision.

Okay, enough of this hyperbole. The real question is this: Why would YouTube do this? Why would some higher-ups at Google decide this was a good idea? Why would all these people purposefully reduce time on-site, increase bounce rate, and willingly annoy millions of users?

By this time, the answer should be obvious: Because it's a joke. It's funny. It makes people laugh.

Here is something fundamental we must impart to you; to everyone, actually. It's a lesson that people understand intuitively because they know the social mores of the society they live in. People understand instinctively, and often subconsciously, what is acceptable and what isn't. They feel it in their chest. They get it without truly understanding why or how, but everyone does get it. Companies, naturally, do not, because they simply *aren't people.*

This is why human beings make sacrifices to help their friends, and often strangers, even if it isn't in their best interest. They know it "works," even though companies do not. It's why human beings make jokes and trust that their friends, acquaintances, and even Twitter followers will "get it," and not be upset. It's why people admit they're wrong, even if it bothers them to do it—yet another act that companies have difficulty with.

There is a lesson behind this. Human beings, when grouped together, intuitively understand how to work in concert. Within a company, groups form that work better than individuals, and inside jokes are normal. People act like people when speaking to their coworkers. It's normal behavior that doesn't need to be questioned or examined. It just works. It's when they interact with the outside that it begins to break down. All of a sudden, when companies speak to the outside, a hierarchy is intimated. We feel we need to speak differently. It's insiders versus outsiders, not like speaking to like.

This is why YouTube's vuvuzela button was a magic moment. It took a risk. At its core, that is what a joke is, and the people inside the company understood this. A barrier was broken down between the usual inside jokes of the company and the outside world. YouTube meshed the two, and by doing so, it appeared human.

In short: This is the secret. In order to be a part of the culture of the Web, you must actually be a part of it. You don't have to try to emulate human behaviors. You have to actually *be human*, in every possible way. Otherwise you enter what could be called the uncanny valley of social networks: You appear almost human but not quite, and that "not quite" throws off the whole equation. Everything falls flat and the illusion fails.

This is why you need this part of the book. It's more important than you think, because as soon as you begin making these public gestures, the way people do and the way your customer does, people who see them will change. Their attitudes toward you will shift. If you make sacrifices, if you tell jokes, if you do all of these things in public, the public will begin to act that way toward you as well.

The Cocktail Party

Quite often, when explaining how the online experience feels, we talk about a cocktail party. We ask questions where the obvious answer is "no," like this one: "Would you go up to a complete stranger at a cocktail party, hand out a stack of your business cards, and ask that person to distribute those cards to his closest friends?" You have to answer no. And yet there's a reason why we have to make that analogy often.

The rise of social networks and social communication is still on an upward curve. At the time of this writing, Facebook has over 800 million users. Google+ (which launched in July 2011) has over 150 million active users. Twitter has over 100 million active users after five or more years. We all use them for different purposes. Some of us connect with friends and families. Others use them for marketing and business communications. It's important to remember that if you replace the words "social network" with "phone," the same is true: We use it for many different purposes.

So back to the cocktail party.

It's important to think about the online version of the human element with the idea of a cocktail party in mind as a litmus test for how social tools help you do business. If you're looking to connect with people and create an Echo between your ideas and their interests, this requires interactions that build a relationship. Let's lay out some specific actions so that this isn't so abstract.

■ From across the room: At a cocktail party, as online, we tend to approach people we find attractive and interesting at first glance. Thus, we dress nicely (or have a good avatar photo) and may be overheard saying something interesting (either through our posts or in something written in our profile information).

■ First contact: When you approach someone at a party, you tend to ask them something about themselves: "I see you prefer red wine" or "I thought I heard you mention that you're a fan of Andy Warhol's work." This is true of the online space as well. What works best is leading with some connective point between yourself and the person you're approaching, whether a prospect or a potential partner. "I see in your profile that you like fly-fishing. Do you get out often?" The opposite, leading by talking about yourself, would be just as rude online as at a cocktail party.

■ Fishing for business: If you're at a party for business purposes, you know how to ask some prequalifying questions. "So you work for PepsiCo? What do you do there?" The person might not be your target buyer, but they might know how to introduce you to the right person in the organization. The same works online. You would no sooner start rolling into your sales pitch with a junior software developer at Microsoft (when you need the ear of a VP of finance to sell your product) than you would in person at a party. Learn who you're talking with and determine how to proceed.

- The gentle prepitch: A cocktail party isn't the right setting to flip open a laptop and walk someone through a Power-Point deck or a demo (sure, it happens, but it's not often the right setting). The same is often true for an online experience somewhere like a Facebook page. What happens in that environment is the gentle prepitch, involving a bit more effort to qualify any interest and then some effort to secure a time to meet (virtually or otherwise) to talk through next steps.

- Introductions: Gold at a cocktail party is when you can introduce people to each other and not have any stake in it yourself. The same is true online. The more often you can introduce two people who have potential future business together from which you extract no further value, the more often you'll find yourself privy to opportunity that seems almost to come from nowhere.

- Going out for a nightcap: At a cocktail party, you can count it a success if you can convince the other person to join you for the after-party. In using online platforms to build relationships, this translates to being able to invite someone back to your main site or offer. If you've built up a good enough rapport and it's obvious that the two of you have something further to discuss, you invite the person back to pursue the rest of the business.

If you look through that flow, it makes sense for how one might conduct business online, at least in one-on-one interactions. The beauty of the online universe, of course, is that some of this takes place without your even being present. People might observe your profile and some of your posts while you're sleeping. Then they might e-mail you because of what they read, which, if it leads to a sale, is business that started while you were literally asleep. Plus, you can carry on far more than one conversation at a time. It's an opportunity to be at cocktail parties all over the world without ever leaving your home.

How to Become Credible

As one of the core factors in Maister, Green, and Galford's Trust Equation, credibility leads the pack. Due to the nature of the Web, most people with Web sites or small companies are nobodies, with little to no credibility, which is one of the reasons they have such difficulty with impact. You might find an amazing article using StumbleUpon or Reddit, but if you don't know whom it's from, what does it matter? We like to think that a strong idea will carry us, and to a certain degree this is true, but the top performers are also always high in credibility, another name for which is *status*. They have accolades. They have testimonials. They have important publications attached to their names and are married to celebrities or whatever.

In other words, they have lots of signals that say they've been around awhile and are trusted by many.

In *Trust Agents* we discussed the well-known story of Donnie Brasco and how he, an FBI agent, infiltrated the mob to the highest levels, seeing things and identifying people in a way the FBI had never been able to do before.

While we told this story, what we did not say, but should have, is that it was possible largely because of credibility. To have a significant impact on any group or culture, credibility is significant because so many people rely on it before giving you any attention. *People* magazine doesn't just give some stranger the front page, after all; its editors need to have seen or heard a name many times before.

In a larger sense, credibility is a necessary indicator for human beings because it prevents society's hierarchies from being disrupted and destroyed. It keeps society stable. Not just anyone can be a doctor from Harvard, because if they could, it would mean nothing. Quality and skill would become largely undetectable, and in a society where strangers are always interacting with one another, we need indicators of quality. Credibility fits the bill.

But how is it really developed? Well, we know from experience that the only real answer is: slowly. The levels of ease with which people feel comfortable with you, from easiest to hardest, are: intimacy/Echo, self-interest, reliability, and, finally, credibility.

So while intimacy is easy to work on, and being liked is one of the first ways you can build Trust, credibility is the most difficult and one of the only ways to reach the top. Credibility is at least partially hackable, in the sense that you can use the names of companies that you've worked with or that have covered your work, or even awards or anything else you've won.

However, credibility is generally a long process in which there is no substitute for continuous, hard work that is consistently excellent. This plays into reliability too.

Quality is the core of Trust. Never forget that.

How to Become Reliable

Even though we said not to, this is the one aspect of the Trust Equation that everyone will ignore. Reliability is hard for lots of people, especially the flighty masses we find on blogs, on Twitter, and elsewhere. Coming up with ideas for content is hard, especially excellent, punch-in-the-face work that will grab attention without resorting to cheap tactics. But it's a necessity. And reliability, ironically, will help you get there.

Rather than using up all your ideas, producing more content

will actually help you create more ideas more quickly than before. If you were tweeting or blogging once or twice a week (or month!), creating stuff every day might intimidate the hell out of you, and rightly so. After all, you think that what you're doing right now is your limit—that it's as hard as you can go. But you're wrong.

Keep in mind that we're not talking here about actually attending meetings you say you're going to, or handing in the presentation on time, or anything else, although those things all matter and will affect your reliability "ranking," if it can be called that. What we're talking about here is creating content, or media, regularly enough that you are seen as a trustworthy and consistent source.

In reality, reliability is all about little stretches. When you begin working online, you'll begin with very little information about how often you should create content, how often you should respond, or anything else. There aren't that many people who will give you direct answers about what's right either. You have to play it by ear and discover what your audience wants. Here are a few things that helped us.

Editorial calendars. You can set these up either personally, on your own computer's calendar, or in a content-management system like WordPress. Planning what you'll publish and when will radically change how you think about content and how you get seen. You wouldn't know it by looking at them, but some of the biggest content creators do this almost like magazines, with months of content lined up ahead of time.

Regular writing schedules. Set up a schedule for yourself for daily creation of content. It doesn't take much time and can help you have breakthrough ideas using any of the methods we've mentioned earlier. Finding thirty minutes a day, or even choosing a certain number of words (such as a thousand a day, as our friend Chris Guillebeau does), will help you produce enough material for everything you own in a very short time.

"3 Tiny Habits." We came across B. J. Fogg's method of habit creation only recently, but his theory is that creating effective habits is itself a habit, and that you can get good at it. To get the full benefit, check out TinyHabits.com, but to start out, find the smallest possible behavior change you can, such as "write one word," and do it immediately after something you already do (such as finishing dinner).

WHAT POKÉMON CAN TEACH YOU ABOUT PERSONAL GROWTH

Chris's daughter is currently obsessed with Pokémon, mostly the trading card game, but also the video games for the Nintendo DS. To participate, Chris purchased his own copy of the video game and played his own version, starting at the same time she did. Along the way, he learned something about improving your impact.

First, let's explain the game's setting and a rough story line, as well as how it's played. If you've played Pokémon on the DS, skip a paragraph or two. If not, keep reading. (You can treat this part as a "choose your own adventure" book!)

In the world of Pokémon, people catch and train different creatures (collectively called Pokémon) for the purpose of staging "friendly" battles. Your character in the game is a Pokémon trainer, and you capture the creatures in various Poké balls and release them to fight against other Pokémon, either in the wild or led by other trainers. Got it so far? You are basically managing a team of differently abled creatures who battle other wild creatures or managed-by-a-trainer creatures in a series of increasingly complex battles.

The creatures earn experience for every successful battle and gain levels after attaining a set number of experience points. The other rewards are financial, but that's not important to the conversation. As your creatures rise in levels, they are permitted to learn new (and more effective) fighting moves, which deliver more damage to your opponent. So, if a level-thirty creature fights a level-five creature, it's reasonably safe to assume that the more experienced Pokémon will crush the other one, usually with one hit.

Now, back to Chris and his daughter. Chris had been training all of his Pokémon nearly equally, giving them each a chance to try to win battle after battle, so his six creatures were all between levels twenty and thirty-five. By contrast, Chris's daughter Violette had one Pokémon at level thirty-five, a few in the high teens and twenties, and the rest around level six or seven. She asked her dad to "level up" all the weaker creatures in her group by making them more powerful, and that's when things started to click for Chris beyond the dynamics of the game.

It would be easier for Violette to just let those weaker creatures go and catch higher-level Pokémon to add to her team than it would be to train each of the weaker creatures. Does that make sense? You could battle for hours and hours with a level-six creature until it grew to a level twenty, or you could just catch a level-twenty creature and add it to your team.

Now, remove everything about that game from your mind for a moment and think about your work, whatever it is. If you're a skilled and experienced musician, do you start a band from scratch, or do you work with people who have a certain level of skill? If you are a reasonably skilled writer, do you partner with a newcomer to write a book? Will you learn what it takes to get to higher levels by surrounding yourself with people who are at a different, earlier part in their journey? Or will that require stretching to learn how to master skills above your current capability?

Whom are you surrounding yourself with right now? If you are an employee, it's not like you can release your coworkers into the wild and capture new ones to do the job better. But then again, does that mean that maybe you've outgrown your workplace?

You can look at this in many ways. Maybe your job is not your calling. Maybe it's just paying you so that you can work on what you really intend to do. Or maybe you're using it as safe harbor between your own adventures. Whatever the case, it's important to realize that you can still do something with the information above, even if you can't apply it directly to work.

Whom do you surround yourself with at work? Are you challenging yourself or learning from them? Whom are you surrounding yourself with outside of work? Does that help you level up? How are you spending your off-hours? Are you at the top of that learning curve or are you finding new, steeper curves?

Whom do you see as part of the journey to achieve your dreams? You have to do the major work yourself, but it doesn't mean you don't have friends, allies, challengers, supporters, and colleagues along the way.

If you've never practiced a single half hour of yoga, then showing up to a beginner class at any venue will probably be a good start. You will quickly outgrow that level and find yourself seeking a bit more of a challenge. Once you reach a certain level with your instructor, you might have to find a more advanced class. It doesn't mean that your instructor is suddenly no good. It means that your goals have shifted beyond what can be attained there.

Chris learns a lot from Julien, from Sir Richard Branson, from Jay-Z, and elsewhere. Julien has most recently learned a ton from Howard Schultz of Starbucks. Along the way, we still maintain friendships with people we knew at different levels of our journey, but at some point we part ways from working with some of those people. As we reach new places in our journey, we require higher-level assistance to grow and succeed. There's a world of difference in learning what it takes to record a podcast than in learning how to prepare your business for sale.

Maintain friendships with those people you consider friends. We're not knocking that. But when it comes to your development, growth, and learning, it's important to level up. Just as you are working on growing your own skills and abilities, by finding connections to people who have grown their own capabilities you are improving your chances of learning what it will take to conquer the next wave of challenges before you.

TRUST: HOW TO RATE YOURSELF

With Trust, you want to rate yourself by thinking through whether people trust you professionally. Because this might be quite variable depending on your situation, we'll give you a handful of examples, and you can extrapolate from there.

Will people reply to e-mails you send? Will they share private information with you? Do people seek your advice? Do you find yourself in arguments more often than regular conversations? Do you get invited into important conversations and meetings? If you're not saying yes, then your Trust factor is low with the people you've surrounded yourself with.

Those few questions might make great measures to gauge people's Trust in you. Seeing the world through a lens of Trust is a decent litmus test for how you interact with the world overall. Earning Trust takes time. It's not like you can show up and suddenly have the interactions you need. This is a good way to look at getting started.

Beyond this, just use the Trust Equation. Any of the attributes in the equation (credibility, reliability, intimacy, and self-interest) will help you gauge how well you are doing and where the deficit may be. Rate each on a scale from one to one hundred and see.

IMPACT EXAMPLE: DOLBEAU.CA

David Gross and David Caplan are the founders of Dolbeau, a small fashion label out of Montreal, Canada, that makes small, exceptional things. From handkerchiefs to neckties to bracelets, the growing label is based on a few basic ideas: Use the best-quality materials, no matter where they come from, and be adaptable.

"I had been reading all of Seth Godin's books when it started to click," David Gross told us, "and the idea occurred to us to make something real, instead of just something digital. We knew nothing about fashion, distribution, apparel, or anything else, but we had a simple idea and we just had to try it."

Fashion blogs had just started getting big when Gross began to notice a kind of trickle-down effect: If you could reach the big fashion blogs, the news of a new product would then roll down to smaller blogs and yet smaller blogs after that. They had an idea to start creating products specifically targeted toward those who were interested in talking about them.

"I was taking marketing and business classes at the time, and I would just go straight home and apply what they had taught me that very day," Gross says. "If we saw 'locally sourced' as a big thing on some of the blogs, we would go and make something like that. If camo started to pick up as a pattern, we would find the best camo materials and make something like that instead. We adapted directly to the trends we saw, as fast as we could."

Within twenty-four hours of its first Web site and product launch, Dolbeau hit the fashion blogs hard. Now it uses apps like Instagram to find fans, connecting directly to those interested in its accessories by giving glimpses behind the scenes of material picking, sewing, and everything else. This insider appeal keeps people seeing its new products, and now the label sells all over the world, sending high-quality men's fashion to countries like Germany, Denmark, Sweden, South Africa, Brazil, and Japan.

How does Dolbeau measure up on our Impact Equation? Let's take a look.

Contrast: By adapting to the exact needs of their industry, and specifically to those who are talking about the cutting edge, Gross and Caplan know they are making something worth talking about even before it trends. At the beginning, their ability to adapt was limited, but after two years in the industry, they are quick and getting quicker. Match that with a passion that bleeds through the site and you get something worth noticing.

Reach: While a tiny label has a small Reach, Gross and Caplan's ability to connect to an audience is actually magnified by the audience whose attention they attempt to capture: bloggers and Tumblr users. They are also adding a blog to the site themselves, hiring the most stylish person they know to talk about fashion directly on their site, making Dolbeau.ca itself a destination.

Exposure: Dolbeau uses Instagram to connect to its fans, so every time a new product or material is launched, everyone knows about it. And because the label isn't selling the same thing over and over again but rather showing a new product each time, the Exposure doesn't seem spammy at all. Further, every week the company release a new limited-edition accessory, which helps bring people back to see new stuff once a week. This is the same strategy used by brands like Zara and H&M to get people coming back and to keep the label looking fresh.

Articulation: Dolbeau's story is easy to sell. It just took 350 words to explain everything you need to know about it. If you are in its target market, you are immediately curious. A clear message helps everything go down more easily.

Trust: As always, Trust is the most difficult to measure. As an up-and-coming brand, Dolbeau is likely low to medium on Trust. It has to build it and get recognized for the good work it does. The experience of using the site is that it is credible, which helps, and its regular weekly editions let you know it will be around, but only long-term consistency will earn Trust. Stay tuned.

Echo: The little jokes on the Dolbeau site help you feel like you're looking at a Web site that people, not a corporation, made. Add to this the slogan on the front page of the site: "Handcrafted. Made fresh. Honestly priced." It's a winner.

Nothing is ever perfect, of course, but in Dolbeau's case, it's always improving. How would you help? What would you change? You can tell the company directly at Dolbeau.ca.

7 Echo, Echo

The British singer Adele performed at London's Royal Albert Hall in September 2011 to a packed audience of adoring fans. The concert was recorded, and we strongly recommend you consider picking it up. It doesn't matter whether you like her music (though Chris does), but it's an education in impact. You see, Adele has mastered many parts of the equation, including how Echo turns her overwhelming success into something even more useful.

The first thing you might notice as you watch the performance is that the audience is quite diverse. There are younger people and older people, couples and friends, children, seniors, and people of all kinds of diverse ethnic backgrounds, all appreciating Adele's music. This isn't accidental. Adele sings songs about love and heartbreak that resonate with people of any age. By "resonate," realize that we mean she's built songs that Echo (echo, echo) the emotions you feel, which helps her grow her platform.

We think the gold in this video isn't in the songs. They're lovely. But what we enjoy watching is how Adele interacts with everyone in between. She talks with people, not as a celebrity but as if they were friends, or maybe friendly neighbors, and she shares how she's feeling. There she is onstage at one of the world's most famous and wonderful performance venues, and she's excited and a bit nervous because it's so posh (her words).

This goes on throughout the entire performance. She talks about what it's like when you have a falling-out with friends. She talks about all the drama of breaking up with someone (her albums are pretty much odes to her exes). Each of these moments comes off as if she's never talked about it in that way before, as if she's talking directly with you, and you can easily relate.

There's something here to think about. If you've ever watched or attended any other live performance, you know that many performers treat their audience as a faceless mass. Sure, there are other bands and performers who don't, but more often than not, you're treated to a variation of "Hello, Cleveland!" for the entire performance.

Adele and others smart enough to work on Echo know that each moment like this is an opportunity to say "you" and mean *one person*. The more you can connect with everyone, one at a time, the better. Whenever you have a chance to show that you are exactly like the people you're blessed to serve (your audience or, hopefully, your community), take it. That's the power move.

This isn't something to worry about when you "get famous." We've seen people at all levels of corporations who forget the importance of Echo and of connecting with the people around them. It's strange to point it out in people with lesser roles, but even as we write this, can't *you* remember a time when someone spoke down to you or otherwise made him- or herself out to be the unapproachable big shot with no real connection to you and your world? Did you ever forgive him or her?

Years ago, Chris had a supervisor who called him and the other three people who reported to her "my staff." Never by name. Instead, if there was a meeting of a few teams inside the organization, this person would say, "Oh, I'm so glad my staff is here. I won't have to take notes." It was as if she thought she was a minor royal figure or something. Oddly (not to you, we bet), she didn't last very long as anyone's boss and made her good-byes a few months later.

How Not to Attempt Echo

This can sometimes go wrong when celebrities attempt to commiserate with people about mundane daily life when it's clear that they're no longer shackled with the same challenges. More than a few ultrawealthy musicians showed up in New York to show their support for the Occupy Wall Street movement wearing ripped jeans and trying to show solidarity. The only problem was that these celebrities were in the same 1 percent income bracket that the protesters were there to complain about. (Mind you, no one was impolite enough to point it out.)

It's hard to go the "I know how you feel" route when attempting to resonate and connect with people. You might not know how people feel. You might not have the same background they do. Then what? How do you show where you're similar without risking dissonance?

What Adele Can Teach You About Success

Let's revisit Adele's performance. She talked about missing drinking with her friends, now that she's relegated to honeyed water. She mentioned how frustrating it is to be the sober friend dealing with the mess that drunk friends create. "I swear she didn't mean it" was one of the "sober friend" lines Adele repeated, to much laughter. This experience was one most people in her audience (and probably you) have had at least once.

Echo is about finding common experiences and using them to help people realize that you have some understanding of their lives. How do you do it "safely"? Well, let's throw "safe" out the window and accept that one might always cause a problem. But here are some pointers.

- Use their language. Making a *Star Wars* joke in a roomful of technologists is a safe bet. Talking about how childhood education has changed since Dr. Spock will at least give you another moment's attention from a roomful of pediatricians. Find their language and use it. Be wary, however, of pulling the Jelly Doughnut. (JFK famously told a crowd of people in Germany, *"Ich bin ein Berliner."* He meant to say, "I'm a Berliner," meaning "I'm just like you people from Berlin." But because he used *"ein,"* what he actually said was "I'm a Berliner," meaning "I'm a jelly doughnut.") Don't use words or terms you don't fully understand.

- Find common ground. When Chris interviewed then chairman of Disney Bob Iger, Bob's first question was "Where are you from?" Chris said, "Maine." Bob asked if Chris had done any sailing around Maine, especially in Searsport. Though Chris has sailed exactly once in his entire life, it was in Searsport, Maine, and on a classic eighty-three-foot wooden-mast antique sailboat. Bob knew the waters there. Chris magically put his only sailing experience into play with Disney's top guy, and the interview went well.

- Share your feelings. This is certainly the opposite of most business advice you get. Feelings are somehow ugly things that should be hidden away. If you're nervous, it is reasonable to express that. If you're excited about something, why not admit it? Sharing prideful emotions can sometimes be dicey, because it can come off as bragging about yourself, and sharing more negative emotions might be frowned upon, but this is one way to build an Echo between you and your audience.

Whether or not you like Adele's music, check out her performance at the Royal Albert Hall, because what goes on between the songs is worth studying and emulating. You might not need the false eyelashes, but other than that, it's all worth taking in. Note, especially, how her audience reacts to her. Pure magic.

The Benefits of Human Sacrifice

There are fundamental aspects to human interaction that most people already understand and that do not need to be discussed. Sacrifice is not one of those things.

Sacrifice is underrepresented in the social sphere because it's thought that interactions have to be win-win, that everything needs to benefit everyone, and that we should always be happy with every single arrangement. Not true.

In fact, it's in lean times that we really start to see who our friends are—those who are willing to give something away when they do not even have enough for themselves. Those who are giving end up being the receivers later on, because they are seen as beneficial to both the community and the individual. They're given preferential treatment because their sacrifice has shown they'll be helpful in the future.

Consider two methods or strategies for being part of community. We'll call one the hoarder; he meets people and guards them from others in order to ensure that he's doing good by his group. He won't make introductions because he's afraid he might look bad as a result of a bad connection.

Now here's another strategy: the prolific connector. He's always finding ways for other people to talk to one another and doesn't care as much how he looks in the process, because he feels that those two people can make their own judgments.

Ask yourself which of these two models of behavior would perform better in a game environment. Which would be introduced more? Which would end up with more social capital than the other? The answer is: the one who is capable of giving—in other words, of sacrifice.

Sacrifice is a fundamental human behavior that showed us whom to trust during times past. If people gave away something, it meant both that they were not starving—that they had high survivability—and that they would take care of us. We trusted these people, and they became our leaders and our friends. Sacrifice helped guide us toward the most powerful, stable group possible. Sharing and sacrifice strengthens groups, which is why we find them in every society in the world.

Sacrifice, giving, generosity, or whatever else you'd like to call it is a fundamental trait in human cultures, and those who do it show signs of long-term potential, while others do not. It's why everyone has faith in bloggers who post regular, amazing content and why we enjoy spending time with people who have lots of dinner parties. All other things being equal, they're seen as givers, which means we feel a need to reciprocate.

Ask yourself how you can incorporate this into your work. Remember that everything you receive is in direct proportion to what people feel from you. Are you telling them, subconsciously, that you are stingy or that you have plenty? Whatever you send out, your audience will react appropriately, so be careful.

I See Myself in You: What Deadmau5 and Paulo Coelho Have in Common

Joel Zimmerman spends his time onstage wearing a giant mouse head and twisting knobs in front of a seething crowd of thousands of passionate fans. Known more widely as the electronic music star deadmau5 (pronounced "dead mouse"), Zimmerman is probably among the top five acts of his kind in the world. Though we like his music, we're more excited to see how he creates Echo by connecting with his fans and turning them into collaborators and conspirators.

On the day this was written, Zimmerman was at it again, this time welcoming people to hang out with him on a live video feed, because he was having trouble uploading a few preview tracks to a site for musicians. Zimmerman chatted with everyone who participated, traded jokes, shared little insights about what had gone into making the songs, and just plain oozed typical human experiences. He kept losing things, physical things, and because everyone has had that kind of a day, it just added to the experience.

Joel also never calls his fans "fans," and he's not one to say "you guys" when he's talking to the group. In short, he works hard on Echo. He works hard to point out that he's a regular guy (well, as regular as someone who has an eight-bit Space Invaders character tattooed on his neck and who tends to wear a giant mouse head can be). It does a lot to leave people feeling like they're part of an experience and not just faces in the crowd.

Now, as promised, let's take a look at how Paulo Coelho is using this technique. What makes Coelho wonderful is that he shifts attention back onto the people who love and support his work. Check out his Twitter background at http://twitter.com/paulocoelho. It's a mosaic of his readers. Look at his responses on any social network and you'll see lots and lots of two-way interactions, plenty of people talking warmly about whatever is of interest to them.

His works stand alone in the way they let readers see themselves in the words. *The Alchemist* has sold millions and millions and millions of copies for a reason. It speaks at a universal level, which is the ultimate Echo. But the person behind the books does a great job of enhancing that feeling by actually communicating and caring outside his books.

This no doubt helps sales, but that's not why Coelho does what he does. He's just passionate about people. It shows through in everything he does, and it's the sign of someone who understands the power of Echo.

A Not-So-Echo-y Example

We decided to look at another popular music artist to see what he was doing to build relationships online (because we don't have much access beyond news clippings to what musicians do and don't do off-line).

It took a while to find a musician who wasn't fond of simply retweeting fan love about him- or herself. When we did, we found musicians who let their promotions people or managers manage their online communications. We're not fans of blasting negativity toward people we feel don't align with our ideas, but maybe we can communicate a few lessons we learned from the musicians we observed:

1. Sharing praise about yourself is a bit silly. Praise others instead.

2. Calling your fans "fans" is putting yourself on a pedestal. Also try removing "you guys" from your vernacular.

3. If you say people matter to you, prove it. Connect and communicate with them. It doesn't have to eat up your day, but allotting some time each day would be a good start.

4. Ignoring people outright isn't a good plan. If your community is really making the effort to connect, respond.

In a weird way the online world has given Echo a new life. For instance, if you still think of MC Hammer as "that guy in the nineties with the pants," then you haven't communicated with him lately on Twitter or Facebook. He's getting a lot of opportunities to do more business because he's become "one of us" through his online interactions. By showing who he is on a daily basis to those who might have an interest, Hammer avoids all the bad jokes and old memories and pushes forward into more and more interesting territory.

As for authors who don't really practice Echo, we've found more of those than we could cram into a set of examples. Many authors seem to save their connecting and communicating for the printed pages. There are many authors who have created accounts on Twitter or Facebook but use them solely for blasting out announcements about the new book, or even less interesting information.

We could find many examples of authors who have thrown away any potential chance to build an Echo. The old method of doing business was okay with this. It wasn't the author's role to market to buyers; the author simply had to meet deadlines (well, you know, try).

For those of you who want examples of what to do and what not to do as an author, here they are:

1. Stop endlessly counting down your book release. Few people are as pumped about it as you.

2. We get just as giddy as you do when people share their bookstore photos. But save the retweets and Facebook shares and the like for praising the followers.

3. Spend even twenty minutes a day communicating with people through an online channel. It's free and it endears you to your buyers and readers. Heck, Chris even wrote about one in this book because she was kind enough to reply.

4. Turn the tables and promote your readers. It will give you a lot more to work with.

Echo is one of the trickier parts of the Impact Equation, but we wanted to give you some thoughts about how deadmau5 and Paulo Coelho are interacting online specifically, because if you want models of how to interact with people and make them feel the excitement of being part of your experience, there are none better than those two gentlemen.

How to Inspire

It would be impossible to talk about building a community and understanding how human beings work without talking about the emotions we want to create with the things we do. It's a basic, fundamental aspect of Echo that we want people to feel a certain way about us, about our brand, or about our content, but unless we really know how to make this happen, we miss out on one of the most powerful parts of creating material online.

Let's face it. There's lots of information all over the Internet about every possible subject. If you want to learn to ride a bike, you can just Google it and *bam*, you suddenly know how. The information isn't what's lacking; it's the motivation, the inspiration, and the faith. That's what you need, not a step-by-step guide. Learning to ride a bike (or anything else, really) is never about the information—it's about the emotion you have to create in order to do it regularly, every day, until it's a habit.

So for us, an inspirational or emotional aspect to our content is critical for moving beyond the race-to-the-bottom, lowest-common-denominator business of publishing on the Web. When you make people feel something, whether it's comfortable, powerful, or any other positive emotion, they associate that feeling, not just the information you've provided, with you or your brand. You get more from them by getting at their heart.

Okay, but easier said than done. How do you actually do that? This is a question we've been working on for a really long time. Julien works hard to make his public speaking about more than just transferring information to an audience, precisely because emotion helps them retain the message better. Chris has worked really hard onstage to make people laugh and has become pretty great at it. Both of us feel that once you have someone's heart, you get the rest of them pretty easily too.

1. Distill your message. Whittle it down to the tightest, sharpest thing possible. And we don't mean something like "Google Panda is making it harder for small Web sites to get and keep high search-engine rankings." If this is what you're delivering, and it's relevant to your audience, that's fine—but deliver a punchier message as well. Use your tone, your words, and everything else to deliver a message that means more to your audience. For example, the message above might become "Big guys are making it hard for little guys to compete." Then your message is more like an eighties movie and less like a horrible PowerPoint presentation. Think ten thousand feet. Think big. Big is emotional, and Google SERPs are not.

2. Discover the core emotion behind the message. For example, for years we used "Don't be afraid to try new things"

as the overarching message of our social-media presentations. Once you have your larger, blurrier, ten-thousand-foot message, you can think about how a message like this is supposed to make people feel. Since there are only a few core emotions, you can basically take your pick, either here or from Wikipedia: hope, gratitude, joy, pride, etc. But remember that a message that doesn't connect with the right emotion can create a kind of emotional dissonance that leaves people feeling not quite right, perhaps even manipulated.

3. Deliver this feeling over and over again from multiple angles. Begin with real subtlety. Create wonder as you talk about how others have dealt with problem X or how great, unexpected successes occurred when person Y was in trouble and did thing Z. Act as if you were telling one of the great stories of mankind through your simple blog post, presentation, or video. Think about building one thing on top of another, not throwing it all out at once.

4. Combine number 3 with detailed examples of how it happened. Don't make the mistake of providing only motivational speaker–type inspirational talk and expect it to consistently work. Your audience needs to feel like there's some grounding in what you're saying. Go from high to low, from general to very specific, and then up and down again. Using examples provides a strong foundation for your subject, and it will help people come along for the ride.

5. Practice . . . a lot. A ton of work is necessary to get seriously good at inspiring any audience, whether online or in person. This is because you need to both anticipate and feel out your audience's emotional state, an ability that comes only with significant experience. So attempting to inspire

weekly, if not daily, in different ways will help you understand what works and what doesn't. There is no substitute.

#

We both have been recently working hard on self-actualization, for
lack of a better term. We have both worked harder at being ourselves, unflinching versions of what we feel and believe. One piece
of advice we have about the process: Package your quirks.

What do we mean by that? There are many unique things that
make you who you are. With a little bit of pruning and positioning, the parts of you that are quirky and different can often separate you from the crowd in a positive way. "Packaging" simply
means putting a little bit of attention and mindfulness into the way
you represent yourself to the outside world.

Meytal Cohen is a drummer in LA who is working hard to
build a platform via online video around her excellent musical
abilities. We came to know her from her covers of various hard-
rock and heavy-metal songs. Think about how utterly niche and
quirky this is. She's an Israeli-born hard-rock drummer in LA who
spends most of her time covering songs and putting them up on
YouTube. Quirky enough for you?

She's doing fabulously, and many other people are finding that
their quirks are a path to success.

Chris's old schoolmate Doug Quint is another example of
someone taking his quirks and running with them. Doug was a
professional bassoonist in the New York Philharmonic but decided
one year to rent an ice-cream truck with business partner Bryan
Petroff and sell unique flavors. But Doug didn't stop there. He
called it the "Big Gay Ice Cream Truck."

With flavors like "Salty Pimp" and "Bea Arthur," not to mention the famous "Choinkwich,"—an ice-cream sandwich made

with chocolate ice cream between two chocolate cookies slathered with, wait for it, bacon marmalade—the Big Gay Ice Cream endeavor is probably one of the biggest quirks-turned-success-stories we can name. Oh, and Doug and Bryan worked hard on platform, using Twitter, Facebook, and a blog to really push their message out to an increasingly rabid fan base.

The Perez Hilton "Hot Mess" Line

There's a line between being quirky and being a wreck. There's a term that we first heard via Perez Hilton: "hot mess." Urban Dictionary defines it as "when one's thoughts or appearance are in a state of disarray, but they maintain an undeniable attractiveness or beauty." This is easy to define in the land of celebrities, but less obvious in the "real" world.

For instance, does it benefit you to share photos of yourself every time you're horribly drunk? Probably not, unless you have a very unique audience. There will never be another Charlie Sheen, who became a kind of antistar for displaying the ultimate public crossing of the hot-mess line.

You might share personal experiences, but how you use that sharing to better define who you are and what you represent to your community will ultimately determine what that sharing will accomplish for you. Again, it's not that you should be censoring yourself, but rather that you'll want to have a better grasp of what it means to share your personal traits.

Sir Richard Branson is dyslexic. He brings this up quite often to partially explain his problem with formal schooling and to make the point that he's passionate about journalism and has written several books in spite of that challenge. This is a great example of sharing a personal quirk (or in this case a kind of disability) that betters the overall story of what Branson brings to the picture.

Just be wary of crossing that line and landing in the "over-share" or "this just got kind of gross" line.

Quirks Can Add Connectivity

Chris loves Batman. He shares this in many ways, including by pointing out that he bought a black 2010 Camaro SS just so he could pretend he owned the Batmobile. Julien loves Dungeons & Dragons and has been playing the game for over twenty years. Every time we mention this, we'll get a message from someone who has a similar passion but hasn't quite shared it with the world at large. You never know what will connect you to someone else.

Here's another odd story of connections that you can file in the "there's really someone for everyone" category. Chris mentioned a quirky, obscure video game called Katamari Damacy and said he was considering buying a PlayStation 2 video-game console on eBay simply so he could play this one game. It turned out there were hundreds of Katamari Damacy players lurking everywhere! As Seth Godin said in his recent book *We Are All Weird*, this is the end of the era of mass and the beginning of the era of niches. So whatever your quirk, package it and lay it out there. Julien connects with many more readers through his mentions of Dungeons & Dragons than he would have if he hadn't mentioned the hobby at all. It's the same with whatever your secret hobbies are—they work for you when they're put out in public, so be proud.

#

If you want one of our best and most secret magic tricks, it's this: Reply. That's it. We know it doesn't look like much, but it's magic.

Julien is better at this in e-mail than Chris is. Chris does rather well in responding to people via his blog and social networks like Twitter. But both of us value replying to people, and it's abundantly clear that when someone receives a reply, they are almost always amazed, for lack of a better term.

Let's be clear. They aren't amazed because we're important (that's not what we think of ourselves). They're amazed because so few people actually bother to reply/respond these days. Yes, sadly, the bar has dropped that low. If you reply to someone, you might actually beat the competition. In poker, this is the same as having a 2 and a 3 in your hand and winning the pot.

This takes work. This takes scheduling. This takes effort. But the act of replying pays off in a way that doesn't fit nicely into a spreadsheet.

Think about it: Have you ever sent a message to someone you thought of as "very important" and received a reply? How did you feel? Which company do you value more, the one that satisfies your needs and also keeps a personable level of contact, or the one that satisfies your needs but isn't exactly friendly?

To be perfectly honest, some companies can get away with not being all that personable. Apple has legions of fans (and both of us are writing this book on MacBook Airs), yet it doesn't do a lot to cultivate the human element of its own Impact Equation. It doesn't matter. We (the combined audience of Apple fans and fervent users) do it for the company.

But you're not Apple. You likely never will be. The rest of the universe has to connect and respond to people.

As magic tricks go, we admit that this one seems rather simple to pull off, and yet people don't do it. Do you? Do you reply to people? Do you respond to e-mails?

Do you know how many e-mail marketing newsletters are sent from e-mail addresses that look like "donotreply@pleasedontre spondtothis.com"? Hint: most. Have you ever tried hitting reply on an e-mail from a company that has sent you a newsletter? Where does it go? Nowhere.

But we think there's value in responding. We think there's plenty of magic in delivering a reply. And we feel that this is actual business value that can be ultimately tied back to dollars, whether or not you can easily track it.

Why does it work? Truth be told, we're not entirely sure, except that in this world of multitasking, apathy, and one-upmanship, the expected response to a piece of fan mail (or any mail) is nothing whatsoever. We can't count the number of times people have sent us e-mails that say, "You probably get this all the time," and end with "No need to answer this, I just wanted to share." No one expects an answer, but when they get one, they love you.

People know that e-mails and tweets take time. They are small sacrifices that imply you took a moment out of your day. They are the opposite of auto-responders that say, "Sorry, I get lots of e-mail." Instead, a reply, even a short one says, "Yes, I am busy, but I actually give a damn." This is important.

Speaking Their Language

If we said our shirt gave us "plus five defense against getting a date," some small group of you would chuckle knowingly. Others would think, *I don't exactly know what you're saying, but I recognize some kind of nerd joke when I hear it*, and a larger group would just smile politely and wait for the book to return to its regularly scheduled program.

All tribes have their language. If you're into Internet memes, you can separate your planking from your owling, and let's not even get into Tebowing. Chris's kids, at the time of this writing ten and six, can each name over fifty obscure little Internet "inside jokes" without breaking a sweat. They know their "Awesome Face" from their "Annoying Orange."

Sports fans can talk about end zones and the shot clock and the crease. Real estate pros can rattle off the definitions of liens and escrow and easements. These languages matter to the people who speak them.

When we talk about "Echo" in the equation, we're talking about how people resonate with your ideas and how they see themselves in them.

We both speak professionally, which quite often puts us in front of very interesting and unique audiences. We've spoken to the glass industry (the people who do everything from making the Gorilla Glass for smart phones to tinting and coating the glass on skyscrapers) to the auto repair and paint industries, to groups of architects and retailers. In every presentation there's a moment within the first few minutes where the audience "sniffs" us with a mix of anticipation, distrust, and near outright rejection. Why? Because we're not "one of them" in their eyes yet, and we can't possibly understand what they are dealing with in their business.

Faced with this opportunity (and it really *is* an opportunity, not a problem), we often find a way to signal that we have done our homework on the industry at hand. Sometimes it's telling an inside joke that we picked up at the cocktail party the night before. Other times, it's mentioning some names to show we've learned who's saying what about the state of affairs in their businesses.

But every time we're faced with this, we reach out for some piece of their language and use it to signal that we understand a little bit about their world.

There's a difference between speaking the audience's language on the surface and really understanding the challenges they face. There's also a difference between empathizing and showing we've done our homework and saying that we know what's best. We prefer to demonstrate that we understand who we're talking to, that we have a sense of what is going on, and that we bridge our ideas to their needs in that way. We never say that we know how they feel or that we've experienced what they've experienced, unless we actually have. There's no benefit in faking it.

Sprinkle in a bit of their language, however, and people will know that you're at least familiar with their world.

Echo in the Workplace

If you speak from the perspective of a frontline employee, why would the leadership ever see you as anything else? If you present your requests, thoughts, and ideas from the mind-set of an outside consultant, why would a company go back to you repeatedly for more help, when others have cultivated their relationships so that they are trusted advisers?

For many years, no matter what his official title, Chris also held the role of "guy who can explain something to the senior team and the technology team so that both get it." After years of working in wireless telecommunications, he was well versed in the world of data centers and large-scale enterprise computing, but through extensive reading and following of the larger business world, Chris also knew how to explain to the chief financial officer why a project was going to cost more due to business continuity planning or what the difference between "having backups" and "disaster recovery" meant from an operations standpoint.

The opposite is also useful. If you're someone who works in the nontechnical side of the house, it's very helpful to be able to communicate in appropriate terms to those you need to interact with to get your ideas across. For instance, if you're talking to the Web-development team about a project, and you don't know the difference between a domain registrar and a hosting company, you're bound to cause some friction. "I bought a Web site from GoDaddy, but nothing's happening when I put in the WWW" doesn't go very far these days.

Echo to the Marketplace

How often have you read in a news article that a leader has "lost touch with the times"? A few months back, Yahoo announced that Jerry Yang finally was completely resigning from the company he founded. A few things that might occur to you when you think about that story:

1. Yahoo still exists?

2. How can a failing company recover without its founder?

3. What will it mean or not mean for business overall?

In the United States at least, the stock market "speaks" in a different language. If a company is making deeper long-term investments, the stock market grumbles. (Jeff Bezos got that for years and years, but he now can point to how that mind-set benefited Amazon's growth plan.) If a company makes a profit but not enough of a profit, stocks go down. Some of the best-loved companies in the world go out of business due to crazy marketplace problems that have little to do with what the company itself can control.

What can you do? Sometimes it's not a matter of just communicating but of speaking in a language they understand. There are many cases of companies turning their marketplace stories around after aligning their ideas with the "language" of shifting marketplace trends. Amazon is actually a good example of this. In recent years (now that people have finally caught up to how Jeff Bezos sees things), it built a strong digital-distribution strategy with its Instant Video, MP3 music, and Kindle book service at a time when shelf space and other overhead costs were crushing its competitors.

Speak Their Language

The Impact Equation has a funny little quirk to it. One element is Contrast (stand out from everything else) and another is Echo (resonate with what someone feels). Don't those two conflict?

Not at all. Do you know how comedians succeed? They create little situations that stand out enough not to be mundane but that resonate with us because we've been there ourselves.

Chris talks about the fact that we all keep our phones really close to our heads when we go to bed, as if we might get a very important call in the middle of the night. It's as if we were surgeons or superheroes, which clearly we are not. This often raises a nervous and resonating giggle. He then strokes his phone as if he's Gollum from *The Lord of the Rings* and says, "My precioussssssss," as people bark out laughter, because they know the feeling.

That, in a nutshell, is how comedy works. Say something that contrasts enough so listeners haven't really heard it said that way before but that still connects with them on some level.

To build Echo into your Impact Equation, it's important to learn how to speak your audience's language and to convey new ideas in a way that almost feels like they were there all along waiting to be discovered. It's a bit of a magic trick, but the rewards are quite lovely, if we do say so ourselves.

About Critics

One thing we should talk about right now is critics. Part of the journey to refining an idea so it has Contrast, building a platform so that you have Reach, and learning about this human-element stuff so that you can Echo the sentiments of your community is dealing with and understanding critics. They come with the territory. They are to be expected and anticipated.

To be clear, these aren't the critics of yore. These aren't people creating a weighed and measured response to your creative efforts. These people often aren't professionals in the field of offering constructive feedback. They are just people who can type and press send. But it's still important to understand their place in the ecosystem.

There's a saying: "Everyone's a critic." It's used quite often in sitcoms and movies, actually, shortly after someone offhandedly puts down the main character's efforts at something like making crème brûlée. But it's truer now than ever before. Now that everyone is a publisher, they all have the opportunity, the ability, and the lack of barrier to voice harsh and unconsidered critiques at the drop of a hat, and they are more than willing to do so around your ideas and your platform.

Eminem and Critics

In a 2011 interview, famous hip-hop artist Eminem was asked whether he managed his own Twitter account. He said that he couldn't really stand to look at Twitter, because he felt that all the critics and haters would get him down. He didn't want to have to answer every negative question or defend himself in every little argument. It's understandable. On that level of platform, with the controversial nature of his ideas, it would be several people's full-time jobs to respond to critics.

Marketing legend Seth Godin says something similar when explaining why he chooses not to enable comments on his blog. He is concerned that he'd spend more time in the comments section arguing little points with people who disagreed than he would spend creating new ideas.

We understand the sentiments of these creators. We have our share of both critics and haters, and it has been quite a journey to learn how best to address them. We have thoughts on that, but first, a question.

Everyone Has a Microphone

One huge difference between the old days of critics and the modern days of critics is this: Everyone has a very visible microphone. Meaning, if someone doesn't like what you say, it can be heard loud and clear. And sometimes, depending on the venue (in this case we mean the online space, but this is also true in the physical realm), critics have access to the same level of platform and volume as the creator sharing the original idea.

Let's say you write a blog post about your best ideas for building business value. Someone can leave a very negative comment with very little effort. This comment is loud, and it's in the "audience" of your post. This person can also write a Facebook message about how wrong you are, a tweet about it, and more. All of these messages are easy for you to see and read. They are hard to ignore, should you want to ignore them.

Now imagine you are onstage, and behind you is a computer screen showing off the Twitter responses to your speech from the audience. Now imagine you see negative commentary streaming by, saying that you're wrong, that you don't know what you're talking about, that you're arrogant, or whatever.

This is new. These feelings are new. Dealing with these kinds of emotions when you might not be used to direct feedback and criticism can be jarring. Think about it. Most employees get direct feedback as rarely as once a year (annual reviews, anyone?).

Sometimes you get little dribs and drabs of feedback, depending on your job. But in the idea economy, not only do you get a lot more feedback, but you get a blend of positive and negative.

A Little Advice About Criticism and Comments

Our best piece of advice is the simplest: Accept all criticism and praise equally as the thoughts and opinions of others and nothing more. This is important on two fronts. First, you can never know the motivations of those providing feedback. Second, both praise and criticism aren't completely helpful, because people will never fully understand your intentions.

There's something else. If you received a hundred comments on something you created, ninety-eight positive and two negative, we know with every ounce of our being that you'll focus on the two negative. Again, none of the comments, good or bad, should weigh very heavily. They should be read, absorbed, and then filed in the "people are giving me feedback" box and given a little less weight than the other ways you evaluate your efforts.

But let's repeat that first point of advice. It would be best if you accept all positive and negative feedback as just the words of others and not take it to heart, but it's important to know that people are voicing their own perspectives on your work.

What to Do with Critics and Comments

No matter what someone says, positive or negative, the most important response you should give to anyone who takes the time to comment (in whatever medium) is to thank them. If you just stop there, that's fine.

This isn't easy. We have failed at this often in situations where the critic ends up getting under our skin. If we get into it, if we get snarky or angry back, we've already lost, because then we're playing the critic's game instead of sticking to our own. The best response is to say thank you and leave it at that.

But what about in a larger business sense? What about when it's more than your ego at stake? Well, there are some professional thoughts about that too.

In a corporate setting, if you have a blog or a forum and someone leaves a negative comment, it's important to have a policy in place that defines your course of action. In our opinion, that policy should be brief and simple, and it should be shared up front with your community, so that they know the rules. You want a quick policy?

1. We prefer words you'd be willing to say in front of children. (You can be angry, but please refrain from cursing.)

2. We welcome on-topic comments. If you seek to protest some choice or action of our company, please see our protest posts. (This would be brilliant to have, wouldn't it?)

3. If you have a negative opinion of us or our company, we'd love to learn from you. Please feel free to leave a negative comment, but also please connect with us via our contact page so we can follow up and try to resolve your issues or concerns.

4. We welcome your suggestions. We can't always please everyone, but our goal is to do our best.

See how fast that can be?
Internally, the rules of engagement are this:

1. If there are curse words, it is preferable to edit those specific words but leave the content of the comment, as long as it's simply a passionate negative opinion.

2. Let's define "on topic" loosely. If they're talking about our company or our products or our competitors, that's on topic. (*Never* delete praise of a competitor's product, even if it stings to read it.)

3. Do your best to follow up with anyone who has a complaint, even if they're "in the wrong" from your perspective. This is a must.

4. Pass on any recommendations to as many people as possible. (Add an appropriate contact list.)

To us, handling criticisms and comments is a powerful part of growing the human element of the Impact Equation. Your mission, and you have no choice but to accept it, is to grow a thicker skin, to learn how to be grateful for any reactions, positive or negative, and to forward comments to the best recipients to encourage response.

ECHO: HOW TO RATE YOURSELF

The name of the game with Echo is to make sure that people feel you're connecting and resonating with them and that your ideas make sense to them. Here are a few questions to consider when gauging your idea's ability to feel so right that people connect to it as if it were their very own.

Do you share the common vernacular of the people you intend to reach? Do you understand their background? Do you communicate in ways that are inclusive of your desired audience? All these things matter and more.

The real dilemma with Echo, however, is that you can't really measure it yourself. Whether you're an individual or a company, you can't measure the touchy-feely aspects of impact from the inside as well as you can from without.

The simplest way to resolve this is to find someone you've known for a long time and someone else you just met, and to ask them similar questions. Here are some examples that will help you gain some understanding.

Do I make people feel comfortable?

Can I look people in the eyes?

Do I talk about myself or about others?

Am I relatable?

Do I let myself be vulnerable around others?

Do I seem relaxed or tense?

These are the measures by which you might judge your success in the land of Echo. Like Trust, Echo isn't something you find overnight. It takes a lot of relationship building to get it just so, lots of experience and error to see what you're doing wrong and right. When done correctly, however, it ends up being among the most powerful parts of Impact.

Conclusion

One big problem when working on creating impact is the trap of the social mirror. We tend to look to others for a perspective on how we appear instead of seeking feedback from within. We get tangled up in other people's perspectives, thoughts, and opinions, and this becomes an issue quickly.

Consider the word "disappointment" or "disappointed." When someone says they are disappointed in us, our first reaction is to feel bad and to suddenly take stock of what we've done to determine just how flawed and bad we are. But have you ever considered the fact that people's disappointment is often their own, and that when they say that, they are really saying, "I'm frustrated that my own internal image of you didn't match with reality"? Has that ever crossed your mind?

Throw into this mix the terms "obligation" and "expectation"; all of these things quite often come from external sources. They cause us to get tangled in other people's issues. For instance, if someone sends you a holiday card, are you obligated to send one back? You might feel like you are, but think about it for a moment. This person has chosen to send you a greeting of some kind. You can opt to appreciate the greeting and take no action. You might also choose to send a greeting back. Make it your choice and not an obligation.

We get tangled up at work too. We think long and hard about pleasing the boss, and sometimes we stop making good decisions because we get too hung up on it. Other times we get tangled up at work by creating rivalry among colleagues. We get tunnel vision over competing for the same raise or for some scrap of praise. But if we step back, we can see that all these kinds of feedback come from outside of us.

When we are tangled up in other people's perceptions, we worry that too much Contrast will make us stand out when we're trying to fit in. (Think back to high school: This was approximately 70 percent of your angst, right?) When we worry about the little things, we chew up a lot of time instead of working to improve our Reach.

It's also harder to be articulate if you're trying to consider the thoughts and social mirror of others around you. You're prone to try to describe things in a way that covers your bases. This obviously also hurts Trust, because if you're trying to be all things to all people, then your ideas get watered down, and that rarely evokes strong Trust. Where you might gain ground positively is in Echo, but that's because you're responding to the sentiments you've seen in the social mirror.

Ways to Untangle

In our conversation about critics, we recommended that you acknowledge all positive and negative external feedback but that you do very little with it. We feel the same here, though it will take even more work. It's a lot easier to distance yourself from the words of strangers and acquaintances. In this case, we're talking about learning how to untangle your feelings and your sense of worth and value from your loved ones, your employers, and anyone else currently wielding power over you.

The goal is to serve the people who matter to you, but only from your own sense of value and worth. Your loved ones, your employer, your customers, and some of your colleagues matter to you. It's great to acknowledge this. Work and live in a way that honors them, and don't worry a lick about the mass of external feedback you receive from everyone, friend and foe alike.

Have you been thinking about specific people? Are you remembering times when someone said something to you and it really hurt? Imagine if that person were somehow instantly in front of you and asked you for some honest feedback about something they were doing. How easy would it be for you to shake off the negative feeling you were just experiencing? How would you judge their effort without bringing in the past?

See how messy this is?

A Quick Reminder: Each of Us Is the Hero of Our Own Story

We all consider ourselves the hero of our own story. Today, when you stopped what you were doing to read this part of the book, you viewed everything that came before this moment as things that happened to you. But go back. Did you have a funny moment with the barista who poured your latte? Did you trade angry e-mails with a competitor? How do you think those people are reflecting on their day? How much of their day are you responsible for affecting?

The answer, almost always, is quite less than you would think.

How the Future Looks to Us

Somewhere out there is a person that has the exact solution to a problem you are having right now. It could be a businessperson. Maybe it's an artist or a student. Who knows? It might even be a child in the middle of Africa.

There are almost seven billion people on the planet, all thinking different thoughts from yours. One of them is bound to have the answer; you just don't know who it is yet.

It would be great if we knew who it was. But we don't, and we won't, because right now, we can't connect to them.

If technology got to where it should be, you would be able to Google your problem and whoever had the solution would be connected to you instantly. They would be able to reach you right away, you would be able to talk about your problem, and they would solve it for you. Or they'd have written a blog post you could read, and it would give you a step-by-step solution, which you would then implement. Everything would fall into place, wouldn't it? But right now, it doesn't.

The ideas in this book will not last forever. They'll only be important as long as people are not totally, 100 percent, connected with one another. At that point, this book will become irrelevant. Everyone will be visible and connected all the time. Everyone will be able to have the impact they should have on the world. Many of the world's problems will get solved at that point—or maybe new problems will be created—who knows?

But we aren't there yet, and we won't be for a while. So this book will help you refine your ideas, which is an essential part of working inside a cluttered idea marketplace where everyone is always shouting for attention all the time. It will help you develop a long-term platform that will give your future ideas a nice place to launch, so they can reach as many people as possible. This book will also teach you how to understand the human element of communication, which is something that people forget when they are communicating in this new way. After all, we are still the same humans we always have been. We should still be thinking about people first, because people will always be the recipients of our ideas.

One day, all of this will be irrelevant. People who discover your ideas will know what you mean when you say them, instantly. Or the Web will connect you to other ways the idea is explained, so that a poorly explained idea won't die but instead will be clarified by someone else.

At some point in the future, the platforms you build will not be necessary. Algorithms will be close to perfect. Now, this future is as unimaginable to us as Google was to medieval peasants. As Arthur C. Clarke once said: "Any sufficiently advanced technology is indistinguishable from magic." So in this future, everything will be "magically" solved, but it won't actually be magic. It will be connection. Good ideas won't die. They will be built upon collaboratively, perhaps the way Wikipedia is today.

At that time, everything will change. But in the meantime, you'll need to hustle. We hope this helped.

The Dramatic Conclusion

If only it were really this easy. The curtain opens, you have your moment in the limelight, and you say your lines. The audience applauds during your solo, there is a love-interest side story, and everything ends happily ever after.

Unfortunately, almost nothing happens this way. This is life, not a movie, so there are no credits that roll after a crisp, simple ending. In fact, if you're anything like us, your life is messy. Not everything fits in quite right. There are mistakes, missteps, and mispronunciations.

Thankfully, as long as you're doing at least *something* right, almost no one will remember them. Instead, they'll remember your home runs and big hits. They'll remember the work that helped them achieve a breakthrough, reach many other people, or make a million dollars. Along the way, your work will spread too. The quality of what you do will improve, and over time you'll become more and more well known. You'll develop a reputation for good work, and it will be well deserved.

But there is never a curtain call and rarely a standing ovation. Rather, when your work is done, the satisfaction lies in the act itself and the fact that you really made a difference. You had an impact on the world. Those who know and look closely will see your fingerprint in the places you labored and in the people you influenced. They'll remember you.

In the world that we're moving toward, everyone will have this chance. It will be taken for granted. We just heard Peter Diamandis speak about the potential and effect of the next billion people to come online in the next few years. What can an extra billion connected minds accomplish alongside the rest of mankind? Their potential cannot be calculated, but their ability to transform the world is unheard of, their impact enormous.

In the meantime, however, the speed at which the world changes is dependent not on the next billion but on those already on the Web: people like you. We hope the concepts in this book help you develop the channel you have always wanted—one that helps spread a message that matters and helps everyone reach the audience they know they can speak to.

Once you have these tools and have mastered them, the next step is to pass them on, to give someone else the ability to leave an imprint. So give this book to someone. It may help them a lot.

Acknowledgments

Thanks to Adrian Zackheim for giving us a shot, and to Jim Levine and his agency for helping us stay on target. Thanks to Rob Hatch and Ron Hood at HBW for helping me find time to write and everything else. Thanks to Jacq for giving this book another read for me. And to Chel Pixie for holding it all together.

Index